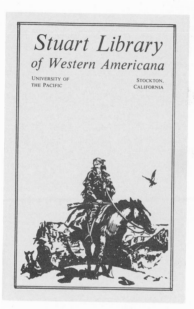

Fort Griffin

on the Texas Frontier

Fort Griffin

on the Texas Frontier

by Carl Coke Rister

University of Oklahoma Press : Norman

BY CARL COKE RISTER
Published by the University of Oklahoma Press
Norman, Oklahoma

Southern Plainsmen (1938)
Border Captives (1940)
Land Hunger (1942)
Border Command (1944)
Robert E. Lee in Texas (1946)
No Man's Land (1948)
Oil! Titan of the Southwest (1949)
Fort Griffin on the Texas Frontier (1956)

and

The Southwestern Frontier, 1865–1881 (Cleveland, 1928)
The Greater Southwest, with R. N. Richardson
(Glendale, 1934)
Western America, with L. R. Hafen (New York, 1941)
Baptist Missions among the American Indians
(Atlanta, 1941)
Comanche Bondage (Glendale, 1955)

Library of Congress Catalog Card Number: 56–10391

To

Watt Matthews

Clear Fork Rancher and Friend

Preface

FROM A POINT near the site of Fort Phantom Hill in Jones County, Texas, the Clear Fork of the Brazos River plows its sluggish and meandering way across northwestern Shackelford County. Then it loops into Throckmorton County and back southeastward across northeastern Shackelford into Stephens County. For most of this distance of about seventy miles the river valley is broad and fertile and is flanked on both sides by rolling mesquite-covered and oak-clad hills, in which rise numerous streams emptying their soft waters into the Clear Fork. Pecan, elm, and hackberry form a continuous tree line along the river like a giant hedge, a delineation which early travelers could see long before they reached it. This L-shaped valley, together with the lower valleys of the river's affluents, may well be called the Fort Griffin country, for an army post by that name established within it was the center of the area's border life and interests for more than a decade of trying frontier experience.

The Clear Fork country was a large part of the Comanches' and Kiowas' favorite hunting ground, abounding as it did in water, wood, and wild game. That pioneer white men also claimed it is yet attested by the tumbledown ruins of Forts Phantom Hill, Cooper, Griffin, and Davis, and by the rubble of what were once stately ranch houses. The region was a sparsely settled and dangerously exposed peninsula pushed into *Comanchería,* a peninsula which federal troops sought to protect, assisted by the state's own forces, the Texas Rangers. Comanche and Kiowa raiders had only to cross Red River and the yet largely unsettled Baylor and Wilbarger counties to reach it; consequently, if they should destroy or drive eastward its settlers, the entire northwestern Texas frontier would collapse.

Distinguished Civil War army commanders—Lee, Thomas, Hood, Van Dorn, Hardee, and Sibley—had gained valuable early experience in helping to defend this settler-penetrated wonderland against the Indians. Within it, also, Captain Randolph B. Marcy and Special Agent Robert S. Neighbors had established the first Comanche reservation; and near by had been built the military post of Camp Cooper to protect the reserve Indians against both their wild kinsmen and encroaching white settlers. On the eve of the Civil War, Captain S. D. Carpenter, commanding Camp Cooper, was required to make a fateful decision of peace or war, weeks before Beauregard's guns were trained on Fort Sumter, South Carolina. Fortunately, he decided to surrender his post without resistance, thereby postponing the outbreak of the Civil War.

"Fort Davis," fifteen miles farther down the river, was the "forted-up" station of Clear Fork settlers seeking protection against wild Indians during the Civil War. Here they were safe. And while here, Sam and Susan Newcomb began their diaries, recording daily such matters as the settlers' monotonous life, their hardships and near starvation, the Indian raids, and, later, the settlers postwar day-by-day trials in and around Griffin or the Flat, which was protected by the fort on near-by Government Hill. A strong federal garrison was maintained at this post for more than a decade.

No segment of the Texas frontier, or, for that matter, of the American border, had a more varied, dangerous, and colorful experience than the Fort Griffin country. Its businessmen, ranchers, and nesters represented wide extremes —the best and the worst. The Flat was classed as one of the West's four wildest towns, giving harbor to unwanted outlaws, whores, gamblers, and killers; but it was also the home town of such enterprising citizens as Frank Conrad, W. S. Dalrymple, Judge C. K. Stribling, H. W. Ledbetter, and members of the Matthews and Reynolds families. Truly it was a cultural paradox.

For a few years not even Dodge City outrivaled Griffin as a border entrepôt; but when its triple source of trade— soldier, buffalo hunter, and trail driver—had vanished, it too folded up. Within two decades it had faded into oblivion.

The Fort Griffin country is one of the West's most nearly unique geographical and cultural entities, a unit about which this book is written. And its present citizens are mindful of their heritage. They have carefully preserved much of their past in varied records—diaries, journals, books, reminiscences, letters, scrapbooks, photographs, and maps—all of which they kindly made available to me. Today Fort Griffin is a part of a state park, which is often visited by school children and citizens to relive pioneer days. And in the Albany City Park are found the old Ledbetter picket house (used as a local museum) and Griffin's stone calaboose. But Albany's "Fandangle," a colorful annual pageant portraying that region's early history, is unique. Robert Nail, a well-known playwright, is its moving spirit.

Albany citizens, to whom I am indebted for making available a considerable variety of materials for this study, for reading parts or the whole of my manuscript, or for assisting in research, are Mrs. Ann Coker, Shackelford County Clerk, and her staff; Miss Ollie E. Clark, secretary, Albany Chamber of Commerce; Mr. and Mrs. John H. McGaughey, *Albany News;* Mr. and Mrs. Ed Dodge and Nancy Dodge; Mr. Watt Matthews; Mrs. Ethel Matthews Casey; Judge and Mrs. Thomas L. Blanton; Mr. Robert Nail; Professor and Mrs. Ben O. Grant; Mr. and Mrs. W. G. Webb; Mr. and Mrs. Graham Webb; Mr. Andrew M. Howsley; Mrs. Ina Wolf Zug George; and Mr. George Newcomb.

Those elsewhere to whom I am under similar obligations are Dr. Neil Franklin, director, General Reference Division, and the staffs of the War Department Division and the Department of Interior Division of the National Archives; Dr. Seymour Connor, archivist, Texas State Library and Archives Division; Miss Winnie Allen, archivist, the Eugene C. Barker Texas History Center, Archives; Miss Thelma Andrews, librarian, Hardin-Simmons University Library; Professor W. C. Holden, director, Texas Technological College Museum; the staff of the Texas Technological College Library; Professor R. N. Richardson, Hardin-Simmons University; Mr. Frank Kelley, Colorado City, Texas; Miss Louise Mooar, Marietta, Georgia; Mrs. Ida L. Huckabay, Jacksboro, Texas; Mr. J. Evetts Haley, Canyon, Texas; Mr. Lestor B. Wood, Breckenridge, Texas; Mr. R.

Preface

Ernest Lee and Professor J. W. Williams, Wichita Falls, Texas; Mr. Don H. Biggers, Quemado, Texas; and Mr. Wayne Gard, editorial staff, *Dallas Morning News.*

I also acknowledge my gratitude to my beloved wife, Mattie May Rister, and to my secretary, Mrs. Mary Doak Wilson, for their unfailing assistance in research, in copying, and in proofreading.

Lubbock, Texas   CARL COKE RISTER

April 6, 1955

Contents

Illustrations

Fort Griffin

on the Texas Frontier

I The Clear Fork Comanches

AT TEN O'CLOCK on the morning of August 12, 1854,
more than forty blue-coated and travel-worn men arrived at
what was locally known as the Fort Phantom Hill crossing
of the Clear Fork of the Brazos, about twenty miles north
of present Albany, Texas. For twenty-one days they had
stumbled through the sterile badlands forming the upper
drainage basin of the Wichita and Brazos rivers and their
tributaries. Within this dreary wasteland these travelers
had suffered from drinking gyp water and a blazing August
sun. Now at last they had come to a land of wild flowers,
green trees, and pure water.

These men were of the Seventh United States Infantry
under the command of a notable Western pathfinder and
explorer, Captain Randolph B. Marcy.[1] Secretary of War

---

[1] Marcy's career had been distinguished by various border experiences. He had been a member of the Black Hawk expedition, 1832; had
been stationed at several Wisconsin and Michigan border posts, 1833–45;
and had taken part in the military occupation of Texas, 1845–56. During
the Mexican War, he had been engaged in the battles of Palo Alto and
Resaca de la Palma, May 8–9, 1846, and had been stationed at Fort Tow-
son, I. T., and at East Pascagoula, Miss., up to 1848, and in Santa Fé,

3

Jefferson Davis had ordered Marcy to explore the upper Wichita and Brazos country for two possible sites for Indian reservations which had been granted recently by the Texas legislature. One reservation was designed for the nomadic Penateka Comanches, who had never before known restricted life; and the other was for peaceful farmer Indians then camping along the Brazos River near Fort Belknap.

On June 1, 1854, Marcy had left Fort Smith, Arkansas, for Fort Washita, Indian Territory, where he arrived after many delays caused by continuous rains, which had swollen the streams above the fording stage and had made the roads impassable. At last, however, he had reached Fort Washita, where he was joined by Lieutenants N. B. Pearce and G. Chapin, with the necessary supplies and a small wagon train. And with this force he journeyed to Fort Belknap on the Brazos River, arriving on July 12. Here Major R. S. Neighbors, special Indian agent, who was to assist in locating the Indian reservations, awaited him.[2]

From Fort Belknap[3] this exploring party moved north-

N. M., and again in Indian Territory, 1849–51. His exploratory work was in serving with Brigadier General Belknap in locating sites for army posts, 1851, and in exploring a wagon road across Indian Territory to New Mexico, 1849; and in ascending the Red River to its source in 1852. See Brevet Major General George W. Cullum, *Biographical Register of the Officers and Graduates of the U. S. Military Academy* (2 vols,, New York, 1868), I, 411. See also W. Eugene Hollon, *Beyond the Cross Timbers: The Travels of Randolph B. Marcy, 1812–1887* (Norman, 1955), 174ff.

[2] Randolph B. Marcy's *Report*, 34 Cong., 1 sess., *Sen. Ex. Doc. 60*, 2; Carl Coke Rister, *The Southwestern Frontier, 1865–1881* (Cleveland, 1928), 37–38.

[3] Lieutenant Colonel W. C. Belknap with detachments of companies G and I, Fifth Infantry, established "Camp Belknap" on June 24, 1851. Later, other units of this regiment arrived to strengthen the post. On

westerly to the Wichita River and, for twenty-one days, were exposed to midsummer heat and consumed by thirst in a drought-blighted area. As they advanced, the region became increasingly barren and uninviting. Here and there was stagnant, undrinkable water in ponds and sand-filled creek beds. For mile on mile the landscape appeared in violent contortions—deep, rock-ribbed canyons; arroyos; tortuous, dry rivers and creeks; and rock-capped, occasionally chrome and gray stratified, buttes and hills, standing in lonely isolation like abandoned medieval castles and battlements.

Marcy described the region as a land of barren and parsimonious soil, affording little but weeds and coarse and unwholesome grass, garnished with several varieties of cactus, most uncomely and grotesque in shape and studded with a formidable armor of thorns defying the approach of man or beast.[4] He thought that the scarcity of wood and water was evidence that the Creator had not intended that it be occupied at that time, if, indeed, it should be populated by civilized man within the next century.

There were no green oases in this region suitable for

November 1, 1851, the fort was moved two miles below the original site, after which the name was changed to "Fort Belknap" in honor of its founder. The drinking water here was brackish and insufficient, although Captain John Pope had stated that the post was admirably located. See Arrie Barrett, "Western Frontier Forts of Texas, "*West Texas Historical Association Year Book,* Vol. VII (June, 1931), 126.

[4] Marcy's *Report,* as cited, 11. Certainly the "breaks" of the Wichita–Double Mountain River country in midsummer bear out Marcy's description. For an excellent day-to-day pinpointing of Marcy and Neighbors' meanderings through Young, Baylor, Archer, Knox, King, Stonewall, Haskell, and Throckmorton counties, see J. W. Williams and Ernest Lee, "Marcy's Exploration to Locate the Texas Indian Reservations in 1854," *West Texas Historical Association Year Book,* Vol. XXIII (October, 1947), 107–32.

an Indian reservation, and so the explorers finally turned about on their return journey down the Brazos River. Traveling eastward, they occasionally saw hill-enclosed valleys with fairly good water, wood, and grass, but curiously, enough, they had been pre-empted by white men.

Before daylight, on August 12, the Marcy-Neighbors party arrived at the divide between the Brazos and Clear Fork rivers, and at ten oclock they reached the road to Doña Ana, New Mexico, which Marcy had traveled in 1849. Marcy later wrote that, a short distance beyond this road, "we entered a section covered with large mesquite trees, beneath which were innumerable large sun-flowers spreading over the entire country as far as we could see, and giving it a brilliant yellow hue."[5] This was Clear Fork country— running streams, rolling grass and tree-covered hills, and deep valleys.

Within this country, agreed Marcy and Neighbors, at least one of the reservations should be established, for here the Indians could find pure water, luxuriant grama grasses, and wood, both for building and for firewood. And, of course, wild game aplenty was found in the hills and along the river. What more could the nomads desire? The Clear Fork Valley was from a quarter of a mile to two miles in width and afforded rich alluvial soil for farming.

Having been convinced that the upper Wichita and Brazos basins were not suitable for reservation sites and that the Clear Fork and Brazos valleys within this vicinity were, Marcy and Neighbors next turned to conferences with the nomadic Penatekas. Both men realized that to corral these wandering Indians on a reservation and to induce them to accept the life of corn-planters would be difficult.

[5] *Ibid.*, 18.

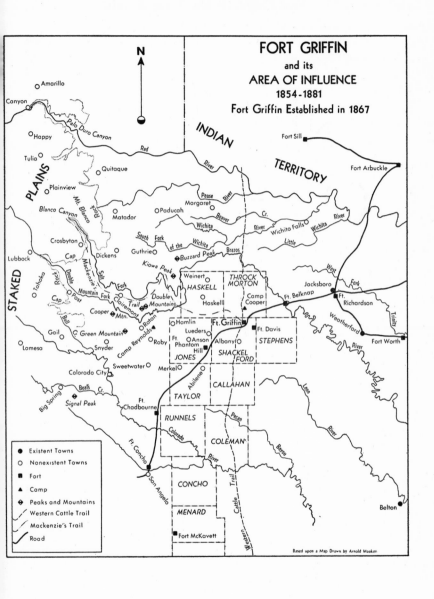

FORT GRIFFIN
and its
AREA OF INFLUENCE
1854 - 1881
Fort Griffin Established in 1867

N

INDIAN

TERRITORY

Amarillo

Canyon

PLAINS

Happy

Tulia

Quitaque

Plainview

STAKED

Blanco Canyon

Mt. Blanco

Rock

Crosbyton

Lubbock

Cap

Dickens

Tahoka

Double

Mountain

Salt

Fork

Cap

Fork

Cooper

Rock

Mtn.

Mackenzie's

Post

Green Mountain

Gail

Lamesa

Snyder

Camp Reynolds

Roby

Colorado City

Big Spring

Beals

Cr.

Signal Peak

Ft.
Chadbourne

Ft. Concho

San Angelo

Red

River

Palo Duro Canyon

Matador

Paducah

Margaret

Pease

River

Beaver

Cr.

Wichita

Guthrie

South Fork

of the Wichita

River

Wichita Falls

Wichita

Little

River

West

Fork

Fort Sill

Fort Arbuckle

Jacksboro

Ft.
Richardson

Weatherford

Trinity

Fort Worth

Buzzard Peak

Brazos

Kiowa Peak

Weinert

HASKELL

THROCK
MORTON

Haskell

Camp
Cooper

Ft. Belknap

Hamlin

Ft. Griffin

Ft. Davis

Lueders

Albany

STEPHENS

Anson

Phantom
Hill

SHACKEL
FORD

JONES

Merkel

Abilene

CALLAHAN

TAYLOR

Leon

River

RUNNELS

Colorado

Pecan

COLEMAN

River

CONCHO

Bayou

Belton

Western
Cattle
Trail

MENARD

Fort McKavett

Sweetwater

Double
Mountains

Raton

Roby

Legend

- ● Existent Towns
- ○ Nonexistent Towns
- ■ Fort
- ▲ Camp
- ◆ Peaks and Mountains
- ⌇ Western Cattle Trail
- ⌇ Mackenzie's Trail
- ━ Road

Based upon a Map Drawn by Arnold Maeken

No doubt, too, both men remembered the previous experiences of Jesse Stem, who had preceded Neighbors as Comanche agent. Stem's agency had been established in the Clear Fork Valley, about six miles below present-day Lueders.[6] This remarkable man had served as "father confessor," peacemaker, and reprover, roles that were difficult and hazardous. Often he scolded the warriors for stealing horses and sought to persuade them, without too much success, to return them to their rightful owners. Ordinarily, the chiefs of the offending thieves winked at their offenses and said that they could not restrain them.

Stem's experiences had been freighted with heavy responsibilities, with constant danger, and with hard work. Frequently, wandering braves visited him to procure supplies, to ask for favors, or to palaver; and always he had employed tact and wisdom in satisfying their wants.

On one occasion Stem had ordered Wichita warriors to return some stolen horses to him, since Major H. H. Sibley[7] with troops from Fort Phantom Hill[8] was visiting the agency and could enforce his demand. The offending Indians reluctantly agreed to do so, but on the following morning they returned only a few of the stolen animals.

[6] Ben O. Grant, "Early History of Shackelford County" (unpublished Master's thesis, Hardin-Simmons University, 1936), 19.

[7] Sibley was a veteran of the Mexican War and had seen frontier duty at Fort Croghan and Fort Phantom Hill, 1853–54. Later, during the Civil War and while a brigadier general of the Confederacy, he led a spectacular expedition against federal forces in New Mexico. Cullum, *Biographical Register*, I, 564; Francis B. Heitman, *Historical Register and Dictionary of the United States Army, 1789–1903* (2 vols., Washington, 1903), I, 886.

[8] Fort Phantom Hill was officially listed in federal records as "The Post on the Clear Fork of the Brazos." It was located about fourteen miles north of present-day Abilene. Brevet Lieutenant Colonel J. J. Abercrombie with companies C and G of the Fifth Infantry arrived at this site on

Again Stem ordered them to surrender those horses with-
held; to make sure that this would be done, he asked Sibley
to arrest and hold as hostages some of the offenders. Sibley
promptly did so, seizing Chief Koweaka and two or three
of his braves.

Koweaka protested. His arrest was an insult and an
outrage. He was guilty of no wrongdoing. But Sibley remained unmoved.

Later, Koweaka persuaded Stem to allow his wife and
little boy to stay in the tent with him. But seemingly this
did not satisfy him; he remained sullen and morose. A few
days later, about midnight, he rushed from his tent, killed
one of his guards, and in turn, as he had planned, he was
shot by the other. Rifle fire brought other soldiers running.
And when they entered Koweaka's tent, they found the
dead bodies of his wife and child. The chief had killed
them, no doubt, with his wife's consent. His disgrace and
humiliation because of imprisonment would have been for
them also a living death.

In 1852, Stem had met in conference such notable
Great Plains chiefs as Pah-hah-yo-ko, Sanaco, Ketumse,
and Buffalo Hump and had received peace assurances from
them. The following winter found their bands encamped
on the headwaters of the Big Wichita below the Caprock,
near the buffalo range. While there, they sent a delegation
to inquire of Stem about the government's policy toward

November 14, 1851, and established the post. His garrison was augmented
two days later by companies B, E, and K of the same regiment. Until the
post was abandoned in 1854, its personnel changed with the varying needs
for protection on this part of the border. Lieutenant Colonel Carlos A.
Waite and Major H. H. Sibley were other notable officers who commanded
the post. C. C. Rister, "The Border Post of Phantom Hill," *West Texas
Historical Association Year Book*, Vol. XIV (1938), 3–13.

them and the advisability of their visiting the Clear Fork Agency. Stem welcomed his visitors and extended through them an invitation to all their people to visit him. He told them that "Father Washington" wished to remain at peace with all the Comanches and to help them in every way possible.

The red messengers were pleased and satisfied with the agent's "talk" and invitation, but replied that their people were many, and that while they would be willing to visit him, he had on hand such a small supply of beef and corn it would not justify their coming. Stem tactfully agreed that he could not satisfy all their wants, and distributed among them blankets, tobacco, "and a small supply of other presents, and sent them back to their people apparently well satisfied."[9]

Much of Stem's spare time was spent in tending an experimental farm, for he did not believe what others had told him—that farming in that area would be unprofitable. He had found the Clear Fork bottom land rich and rainfall sufficient to grow crops. So he decided to plow and plant a treeless area near the agency. Marcy said that Stem's "experiment was made by turning over the sod with a prairie plow, and planting the seed [corn and oats] upon it." No other labor was expended in the way of hoeing or plowing, but the crops grew luxuriantly and produced a bountiful yield of grain.[10] Stem met with pronounced success for three successive seasons and found a ready market for all his grain at Fort Belknap.

[9] Stem to Lea, March 31, 1853 (Copy of the letter in Indian Office records of the National Archives supplied from the R. N. Richardson Collection, Hardin-Simmons University).

[10] Randolph B. Marcy, *Thirty Years of Army Life on the Border* (New York, 1866), 208.

But Stem's life was about ended. Shortly he resigned his Indian agency and engaged in farming near Fort Belknap. During the winter of 1854, when he and an Ohio friend, Lepperman, were riding to Fort Belknap, about ten miles away from the post, they were murdered and their bodies mutilated. For several weeks the local authorities could obtain no clue as to how they met their death.

A short time later some Kickapoo Indians, while visiting Fort Arbuckle, about five miles west of present-day Davis, Oklahoma, reported to the commanding officer that Kickapoo renegades were the murderers, although this tribe was at peace with the whites. Immediately, the commandant sent for their chief, Mosqua, and when Mosqua arrived, informed him of what he had heard. The chief replied that a boy of his tribe had previously brought him this news. The lad had told him that recently he had gone to the Brazos River in Texas with two warriors and had seen them kill two white men. Mosqua had sought to arrest the accused men, but they had made their escape, and his tribesmen were still searching for them. Before leaving Fort Arbuckle, he assured the commandant that the guilty men would be brought to justice.

In the *Journal* of L. Glisan, a Fort Arbuckle medical officer, and in Marcy's report of 1854 is recorded the final solution of the case. Glisan wrote on March 18, 1854, that Waco Indians had reported that Kickapoo warriors had acted suspiciously. The previous evening they had come to Nelson's trading house, twenty-seven miles from Fort Arbuckle, to sell some trace chains. They also "had several uniform coats and quite a lot of money." But when Black Beaver, a well-known Delaware scout at the fort, heard the Wacos' story, he identified this party as Dela-

11

wares, who had obtained these articles from the Fort Arbuckle quartermaster. He added, however, that several
Kickapoos had told him that one of their tribe, Sa-kok-wah
(alias "Morgan" or "Polecat"), and a one-eyed half blood,
Pe-a-tah-kak (a half-blood Kickapoo, Pi-an-ke-shaw), accompanied by the former's brother-in-law, a little boy, had
just returned from the Texas Brazos country where they
had murdered the two white men.

Mosqua now made every effort to arrest the guilty Indians. He sent out a party of his braves, who succeeded in
arresting Pe-a-tah-kak and returning him to the Kickapoo
village. Mosqua had him bound with ropes, put on a horse,
and sent under heavy guard toward Fort Arbuckle; but before reaching there, Pe-a-tah-kak drew a knife which he
had concealed in his leggings, cut his shackles, and attempted to flee, and one of the accompanying horsemen
instantly killed him. The warriors threw his corpse on a
horse and carried it on to the fort.[11]

Meanwhile Mosqua made a public appeal for the arrest or the killing of the other murderer. Should any white
man meet a single Kickapoo out by himself in any direction,
ran the appeal, he was authorized to shoot him down without hesitation.

Just here Marcy[12] added colorful detail to the Glisan
account. "Several days elapsed without any news of the
fugitive," he wrote, "but at length a runner came in and
communicated the following facts: It appeared that on

[11] L. Glisan, *Journal of Army Life* (San Francisco, 1874), 133ff.

[12] *Ibid.*, 141, 142. Glisan stated in his journal entry of June 13, 1854:
"Captain R. B. Marcy is daily expected on his way for the frontier of
Texas" (p. 141), and on June 21, "Captain Marcy arrived here on the
twenty-fourth with an escort of forty men, under Lieutenant N. P. Pearce"
(p. 142).

leaving his own village the murderer had made his way to another camp upon the Canadian river where he had a brother living.[13]

"As he [the murderer] passed along through the camp in going towards the lodge of his relative, he exclaimed in a loud voice: 'I am the man who killed the two white men near the Brazos river, and if anybody wishes to take my life, here I am. I am not afraid to die.'

"No one molesting him, he entered the lodge, saying to his brother as he did so: 'Here you see me, my brother, a fugitive from justice. My own people are upon my trail; I am hunted down like a wild beast. I am like a wounded deer that cannot escape. I would have gone and sought the protection of the wild Indians, but was fearful I should starve before I found them. There was no place where I could go, else I come to you.'

"After partaking of a supper that was prepared by him, and talking with his brother for some time, they walked out together and had proceeded a short distance outside the camp, when the brother stepped behind him, raised his tomahawk, and with a single blow felled him to the earth.

"He then seized him, saying: 'I have often warned you, my brother, of the consequences attending the course of life you have been leading, and told you it would ultimately bring you into trouble and disgrace. You have rejected my counsels, violated the laws of the United States, and thereby brought the displeasure of the whites upon your tribe, and they demand ample reparation for the deed you have committed.'

[13] At this point in the narrative, Marcy's paragraph structure is changed for better reading; the sentences are unchanged.

" 'You have forfeited your life,' he continued, 'and it now becomes my painful duty to kill you.'

"He, therefore, deliberately put him to death, and reported the facts to the chief, who forthwith assembled a council, and it was determined, as the distance to the fort was too great to transport the body, that the head should be sent to establish the identity of the individual killed, which was accordingly carried into execution, and the head exhibited to the commanding officer at Fort Arbuckle on the following day."[14]

Thus the murder of Agent Stem and his companion was avenged. Marcy rightly stated that Kickapoo justice evinced "a regard for law, and an inflexibility of spirit in the execution of its mandates, seldom found among any people."[15]

Both Marcy and Neighbors used their knowledge of Stem's experiences on the Texas frontier in negotiating with the Comanches. Stem had gotten along well with the Comanches, and had influenced them for peace. Moreover, he had proved that the Clear Fork was farming country.

In conferring with the Comanches, Marcy and Neighbors found that there was jealousy and ill will between Ketumse and Sanaco. Ketumse had told the white men that he spoke for all the Comanches, but when Sanaco heard of this claim, he sent two messengers to Marcy asking him to put no confidence in Ketumse's "talk." In fact, as early as August 21, 1852, Sanaco had addressed a letter to "Messrs. T. Howard and all whom it may concern—" in

[14] It should be remembered that his dialogue is not faithfully verbatim. The general account is no doubt as it was given to Marcy by the Indians and fellow officers when he arrived at Fort Arbuckle a few days later on his way to Fort Belknap.

[15] 34 Cong., 1 sess., *Sen. Ex. Doc. 60*, 39.

14

which he asked "conclusively . . . please to look into the matter as it stands now between me and Ketumsee, I am tired of being abused by him continually and with such impunity." He said that Ketumse had told the commanding officer on the San Saba to send soldiers to bring him down, to take everything from him, or "to fight me and kill me off."[16] With such a long-standing feud between the two chiefs, Marcy no doubt found it difficult for them to agree on matters now.

So, on August 20, Marcy assembled Sanaco, several subchiefs, and a chief of the Middle Comanches in a final conference where the California road crossed the Qua-qua-ho-no (Paint Creek). He warned the Indians that if they did not accept the Great Father's terms they would soon come to want. Within a few years nature's commissary, upon which they had depended, would be gone. The buffalo and the deer would disappear, and the warriors and their people would have to seek subsistence elsewhere. If they now accepted his terms, Father Washington would send them farmers to show them how to raise corn and other crops, and would supply them with agricultural implements, and with provisions until they could raise their first crops. Their agent would see that they were not molested by the whites, and their rights would be respected by neighboring brethren. But for these benefits the government would expect them to obey its orders and to remain firm friends of their benefactors.

Ketumse had previously found Marcy's "talk good," and now Sanaco also accepted it. Both were ready to bring their people to the new reservation when it was created.

[16] Robert S. Neighbors Papers, 1857–59 (MS Division, University of Texas Library).

Neighbors strengthened Marcy's promises by distributing presents and rations among the Indians, whose camps that night were alive with feasting and revelry.

Marcy and Neighbors quickly agreed upon two reservations. The Comanche reservation of four leagues was surveyed in the valley of the Clear Fork and on the present Throckmorton County side of the river and a few miles above the future site of Fort Griffin. It was a fine, arable tract of land, although the village site was occasionally inundated when the river overflowed its banks.

Previously, Chief José María of the Hainais and Anadarkos, Tiner of the Caddoes, and Cack-a-quash of the Tawakonis had told Neighbors that they much desired a permanent home near Fort Belknap where they would be free from interruption by white men who chose to claim their lands. Always in the past the white men had come to oust them after they had improved their holdings. But they would not accept any reservation which he and Marcy might select in the upper Wichita or Brazos country, for there they would be at the mercy of the wild tribes. During past summers the Comanches had visited them only to eat their green corn and to take their cattle and crops. No, unless they were located below Fort Belknap, where they would have federal protection, they would take the consequences; they would remain where they were, and die with full bellies! So when Marcy and Neighbors had returned from their reconnaissance in August and had told the anxious Brazos chiefs that their reservation would be located below Fort Belknap, they immediately accepted it.[17]

Both federal and state officials were pleased. These

[17] 46 Cong., 2 sess., *Sen. Ex. Doc. 74*, III, 26f.; *Annual Report of the Commissioner of Indian Affairs, 1859* (Washington, 1860), 234.

Lieutenant Colonel Robert E. Lee

two reservations might be the beginning of the solution of the Indian problem and the end of border raids. If these experiments were successful, other Indian bands might also be encouraged to undertake reservation life. But before the end of another year these hopes gave way to fears.

The Comanches along the Clear Fork awaited anxiously the fulfillment of Marcy's and Neighbor's promises; they could not understand why the Great Father delayed making their reservation available. In September, the newly appointed Special Agent G. H. Hill of the Comanches reported to Neighbors in San Antonio that he had just returned from a twelve-day trip to the Indian country, where he had found the Indians anxious to move to their reservation to learn about the white man's farming and institutions.[18] Three months later he again urged Neighbors, now the superintendent of the Texas Indians, to hasten reservation arrangements. Accompanied by Lieutenant A. D. Tree and a detachment of Dragoons, he had recently visited the Clear Fork villages of the Penateka chiefs, who had told him of their desperate condition. They said that they were pressed on one side by advancing white settlements and on the other by the Northern Comanches, who had often come to their villages with stolen horses and had encouraged them to join in raids. Since they had depended on Marcy's promise of food, which had not been given, they now were in great need.[19]

Such reports from the frontier at last brought action. On January 8, 1855, Neighbors wrote to Commissioner of

[18] Hill to Neighbors, September 20, 1854 (MS in Letters Received from Texas Agencies, 1854–55, Pt. I, O.I.A., National Archives, Washington).

[19] *Ibid.*, December 15, 1854.

Indian Affairs George W. Manypenny that on November 10 of the previous year he had left San Antonio for western Texas, where eight days later, at Fort Chadbourne, he had talked to a small party of Comanches, who had told him that they were from the main Comanche camps along the Clear Fork, fifteen miles below the reservation selected for them. Consequently, he had visited them—all the Southern Comanches (Sanaco's, Ketumse's, and Buffalo Hump's, or from one thousand to twelve hundred men, women, and children), among whom he distributed beef and corn which he and Special Agent Hill had purchased at Fort Belknap.[20] He said that the chiefs had urged him to hasten the completion of reservation matters; and, in his opinion, unless this were done, the starving Indians might again resort to depredations.

But at last both reservations were made ready for occupancy. The Fort Belknap reserve was opened to its farmer bands—188 Caddoes, 205 Anadarkos, 94 Wacos, 136 Tawakonis, and 171 Tonkawas, or a total of 794 Indians, the members of which were soon busily engaged in clearing their farms.

While waiting for the opening of the reservation, the Penatekas had become restless; rumors were in the air. A German trader had sent a messenger to Sanaco on the Clear Fork to say that a strong white army was advancing from the south to destroy the reservation. Promptly, Sanaco and Buffalo Hump and all their people had decamped in great alarm. The report had some basis of fact. Actually, troops under Captain Patrick Calhoun were moving up from Fort Chadbourne to destroy or drive northward those nonreser-

[20] 46 Cong., 2 sess., *Sen. Ex. Doc. 74*, III, 26f.; *Annual Report of the Commissioner of Indian Affairs, 1859*, 234.

vation Northern Comanches and Wichitas who had been raiding along the frontier. Calhoun told Hill, however, that he had been ordered to attack *all* Comanches wherever they might be found and that he expected to do just that.[21] It is doubtful, however, that he would have molested the Clear Fork Comanches had he encountered them.

Nevertheless, Hill thought the expedition was a grave mistake. Why would not the federal military authorities help him solve the Indian problem by peaceful means? "Half a million dollars," he wrote Neighbors gloomily, "will not produce the same quiet and calm condition of the Indian mind that existed on the frontier forty days ago."[22]

Ketumse alone had refused to be stampeded. He believed that the trader's report was false and so advised his people. They did not leave the reservation, although some of the young braves were restless and disgruntled.[23]

[21] Lena Clara Koch, "The Federal Indian Policies in Texas," *Southwestern Historical Quarterly*, Vol. XXIX (July, 1925), 21–22.

[22] Hill to Neighbors, Feb. 12, 1855.

[23] R. N. Richardson, *The Comanche Barrier to South Plains Settlement* (Glendale, 1933), 23.

II The Perilous Agency

By JANUARY, 1856, a newly organized crack United States Cavalry regiment was on the march to bring stability to the Clear Fork country. This regiment,[1] under the command of Colonel Albert Sidney Johnston,[2] had marched from Jefferson Barracks, Missouri, through Indian Territory and then southward via Fort Washita and Fort Belknap, to the Clear Fork, where it arrived on January 3, to begin its occupation of Camp Cooper, two miles above

[1] The Second Regiment of Cavalry was organized by act of Congress on March 3, 1855. Heitman, *Historical Register and Dictionary*, I, 71.

[2] Johnston was one of the most celebrated officers on the Texas border during this period. He graduated from West Point in 1826, served in the Black Hawk War of 1832; as adjutant general of the Army of the Republic of Texas, 1836; as Texas senior brigadier general, 1836–38, and secretary of war, 1838–40; and in the Mexican War, 1846–48. He was a farmer on the Brazos River, 1846–49; appointed a colonel in the Second United States Cavalry, 1855; stationed on the Texas frontier and at Headquarters, Department of Texas, 1856–57; commanded Utah expedition, 1857; and was in command of the Department of the Pacific, January to April, 1861, when he resigned to enter the service of the Confederacy. He was killed on April 6, 1862, at the battle of Shiloh, while commanding the Southern Army. Cullum, *Biographical Register*, I, 291.

Ketumse's village.[3] The new post was named in honor of Adjutant General Samuel Cooper.

Johnston did not tarry long; he moved on southward to Fort Mason, via Fort Chadbourne, leaving Major William J. Hardee[4] and two squadrons of his regiment to man the new post.

Yet Hardee's command of Camp Cooper was only temporary; on April 9, Lieutenant Colonel Robert E. Lee[5] arrived to take his place. Lee, fresh from his superin-

[3] Colonel James K. F. Mansfield's "Inspection Report" of the Department of Texas, April–August, 1856 (MS, Records of the War Department, A. G. O., Misc. File, No. 282, National Archives, Washington). The agency buildings were eighteen in number and made of "drop logs" or pickets.

[4] Hardee graduated from West Point in 1838. He served with the Second Dragoons from 1838 to 1846; in Mexico, 1846–48, where he was twice cited for meritorious conduct in battles of Medelin and San Augustine, being breveted major and lieutenant colonel respectively. He was on frontier duty in Texas for almost the entire period 1848–56, and on the later date he came to Camp Cooper as a major of the Second Regiment of Cavalry. During the Civil War, he was conspicuous as a Confederate Commander under General Robert E. Lee. Cullum, *Biographical Register,* I, 561.

[5] Lee visited Texas first in 1846 as a captain and chief engineer of General John Wool's army preparing to invade Mexico. Later, he was a much trusted and praised young officer in General Winfield Scott's army on its march from Vera Cruz to Mexico City. After the war, Scott referred to Lee as America's "very best soldier." In 1848, Lee was assigned to special duty in the Engineer Bureau, and for the next two years he was a member of the Board of Engineers for Atlantic Coast defenses. Meanwhile, he became the superintendent of West Point, 1852–55. Next, he commanded Jefferson Barracks, Missouri, 1855, after which he returned to Texas as a lieutenant colonel of the Second Cavalry and as commandant of Camp Cooper, 1856–57. His other services in Texas were as commander of the Military Department of Texas and as commandant of Fort Mason (1860). He became a colonel of the First Cavalry on March 16, 1861, but resigned his commission a month later to enter Confederate service and became the South's most distinguished commander in the war which followed. Heitman, *Historical Register,* I, 625; Cullum, *Biographical Register,* I, 338.

tendency of West Point, was hardly conditioned in mind to acclimate himself to the raw Texas frontier. On the day following his arrival, Ketumse, dirty and smelly, called to pay his respects. Lee did not appreciate his generous hug and presently wrote to his wife, Mary, at Arlington, Virginia, that his Comanche charges were "extremely uninteresting," and that this reservation experiment was ill advised.[6]

At Camp Cooper, Lee felt that he was sidetracked "in a desert of dullness from which nothing is drawn." Here he would have no chance of promotion and would be far removed from Mary and the children. Moreover, his new experiences were trying in the extreme. Drought had blighted the land, Camp Cooper was but a collection of tents on a poorly chosen site, and sandstorms plagued the camp one week and dry northers the next.

In time, however, Lee wrote affectionately of his "Texas home." Lonely rides along the Clear Fork and visits in the homes of widely separated ranchers brought him peace of mind and a measure of contentment. On one ride, he procured milk, butter, and eggs at a ranch; at another, a spotted cat, about which he wrote to his baby daughter, Mildred. He also added teasingly: "My rattlesnake, my only pet, is dead. He grew sick and would not eat his frogs and died." In fact, however, rattlesnakes made life hazardous about the post. Because of them, Lee had to build a coop for his chickens well above the ground.

Still, Lee found little time for annoyances. His days were filled with letter-writing and reports, with court-martial duty, with inspecting the near-by country for a more

[6] Lee to Mary Custis Lee, April 12, 1856 (MS in Lee family papers, Library of Congress, Washington).

favorable site for his post, with directing the movements of frontier patrols, and with leading an expedition against marauding Comanches in the Double Mountain country.[7]

Presently, when a court-martial session was to be held at Camp Cooper, Lee was in great distress; Major George Thomas and his wife were to come to the Clear Fork. Lee could put up with army fare—for breakfast, Dutch oven biscuits, occasionally eggs, molasses or stewed peaches and apples; for lunch and dinner, boiled beef, potatoes, beans, canned fruit, and bread—but Mrs. Thomas must have more. Only recently in San Antonio she had served him an elaborate breakfast and luncheon.[8] "The supper last night was so good," he had written Mary, "and so much to my taste, venison steak, biscuit and butter, that I had little appetite for breakfast, though waffles, eggs, and wild turkey were three dishes that it presented; and when the dinner of wild turkey, tomatoes, French peas, snap beans, and potatoes, was followed by plum pudding, jellies and preserved peaches, I despaired of eating any of Mrs. Smith's supper."

To add to his army fare, Lee sent his cook, Kremer, to procure butter, milk, and poultry at the nearest ranch, perhaps Givens'; but Kremer returned with only "a few eggs, some butter, and one old hen," Lee wrote Mary despairingly. He would write soon how he "got on" with the entertainment of his dainty guest; but he must have succeeded fairly well, for he did not address Mary again on this subject.

[7] Carl Coke Rister, *Robert E. Lee in Texas* (Norman, 1946), 37ff.; Lee to Major D. C. Buell, assistant adjutant general, Department of Texas, San Antonio, July 24, 1856 (MS in Letter Book, No. 2, Lee family papers, Library of Cong., Washington); Lee to Mary Custis Lee, July 28, 1856.

[8] He had had supper with Colonel and Mrs. Albert Sidney Johnston and breakfast and dinner with Major and Mrs. George Thomas. See Lee to Mary Custis Lee, April 27, 1857.

On May 27, 1856, the departmental commander ordered Lee to head an expedition against Sanaco's band and
other hostile Indians, supposedly near the Big Spring.
These Indians had refused to accept the Clear Fork reservation and were raiding the settlements. Lee was to explore
the region as far westward as the Double Mountain, but
he was to use his own discretion as to the route. He was
also to furnish a map of the country covered.

Lee was not successful in his expedition against the
Nokoni, Tanima, and Penateka Comanche raiders, for they
were far to the north hunting buffalo. Although he had
made a wide swing via Fort Chadbourne out to the Double
Mountain and return, a journey of eleven hundred miles, he
found and punished only one small band of marauders who
were returning from a raid in Mexico, and he brought back
to the post only an Indian woman as captive.[9] In later
months there were Indian scares, one in the night. On
this occasion the Camp Cooper garrison was greatly excited and made preparations to repel an attack, but Lee
slept on in his tent. Well he might, for the Indians did not
molest the post.

Although Lee's stay at Camp Cooper for the next few
months was uneventful, the days of the near-by Indian
agents who succeeded Hill were perilous and filled with
trouble. Non-agency Indians frequently used the reservation as a base from which to project thieving raids along
the frontier,[10] and sometimes they were aided by reserva-

[9] *Ibid.*, July 28, 1856.

[10] Buell to Lee, May 27, 1856 (MS in Letters Received, Department
of Texas, Records of War Department, A. G. O., 185–T–1856, National
Archives, Washington); Captain N. G. Evans to Captain John Withers,
assistant adjutant general, San Antonio, January 14, 1858 (MS in Letters
Received, Department of Texas, Records of War Department, A. G. O.

tion warriors. In turn, angry settlers followed the Indians back to the reservation, on which unauthorized whites were not permitted. This led to increasing friction between the settlers and the Camp Cooper military and civil authorities.

In August, 1858, Santa Anna, a notoriously "bad Indian," with a Nokoni warrior, stopped at Ketumse's village. Ketumse ordered these unwelcome visitors to leave, but they refused. Then he called upon Lieutenant Cornelius Van Camp's troopers to expel them, but the reservation Indians, observing the usual Comanche courtesy to village guests, rallied to Santa Anna's support. Ketumse made an issue of the occasion. "Too much talk no good," he exclaimed, and sprang forward as if to enter the house where the visiting Indians had sought refuge. But he was violently seized by about thirty women, who in tears begged him not to proceed.

Ketumse then asked all who were his friends to line up with him beside Agent Leeper and Van Camp. Only his brother and nephew, an old Indian named "Hawk," and two others did so, "while the remainder, numbering some seventy warriors and thirty women and boys who could use arms, placed themselves opposite us with bows strung and rifles leveled." It was then that Van Camp's sergeant told him that he had only one round of ammunition, so, in vexation, Van Camp was forced to withdraw his cavalry.[11] Subsequently the reservation Indians were mollified when they

National Archives, Washington). Captain Givens had reported that horses stolen from his ranch had been found on the Camp Cooper reservation.

[11] Leeper to Neighbors, August 31, 1858, in 35 Cong., 2 sess., *Sen. Ex. Doc. 1*, II, 264–65; Leeper to Neighbors, August 21, 1858 (MS Division of War Records, A. G. O., National Archives, Washington).

learned that Ketumse and Van Camp were only trying to serve the best interests of their village.

But conditions at the agency "went from bad to worse." Raiders continued to use the reservation as a sanctuary, and when the settlers accused Ketumse's braves of thieving, both the local military and civil authorities demanded proof. The settlers, in turn, charged the reservation officials with condoning, and even abetting, the raids. John R. Baylor, formerly a Clear Fork agent,[12] held the commonly accepted belief that "all good Indians are dead ones," and was the antireservation leader.

In the spring of 1859, Baylor led a strong settler force westward to destroy the reservation, but troops at Camp Cooper prevented him from doing so. This did not stop the angry settlers; other parties of border men ranged the country looking for roving Indians. One of these, on December 5, 1858, attacked Choctaw Tom's camping party of peaceful Anadarkos and Caddoes near Ritchie Creek, a few miles below their reservation, and killed seven and wounded the rest.[13]

Of course, Camp Cooper authorities condemned this "wanton massacre," which it truly was; but the settlers, already aroused because of recurring raids along the border, replied that these were thieving Indians and demanded that the near-by reservations be abandoned. They held

[12] Baylor had been dismissed from the service, probably because of Neighbors' recommendation, in 1857, and was succeeded by Matthew Leeper in May, 1857, who remained as agent until the Comanche reservation was abandoned two years later. Richardson, *The Comanche Barrier to South Plains Settlement*, 222, 248.

[13] *Annual Report of the Commissioner of Indian Affairs, 1859*, 234; 36 Cong., 1 sess., *Sen. Ex. Doc. 2*, I, 588.

meetings in frontier towns and communities east of the agency to ask the Governor and President to do away with the Clear Fork reservation. In August, 1859, the Commissioner of Indian Affairs so ordered.

Now defeated and despondent, Neighbors rounded up his charges and started for the Red River, escorted by Major Thomas with companies "G" and "H" of the Second Cavalry and a detachment of infantry. The dispirited Indians were taken to Fort Cobb, Indian Territory. Several years later, the Wichita Reserve agent in this area wrote that the sorry handling of the Texas reservations was the principal cause of increased Comanche raids on Texas.

Then Agent Robert S. Neighbors, who had found his Indian agency perilous, like Jesse Stem, fell mortally wounded from a murderer's bullet—*not* from the gun of an agency Indian. In 1859 he was treacherously slain at Fort Belknap by a white outlaw.[14]

On September 14, 1859, William Burkett, no doubt serving in a judicial capacity, wrote Mrs. Neighbors the particulars of her husband's death. The preceding day, Neighbors, accompanied by Agent Leeper and his family, Mrs. Charles E. Barnard, Captain Ross, and about six or eight more persons, had arrived at Belknap on the return trip from taking the Texas reservation Indians north of the Red River. On the morning of the fourteenth, Neighbors had entered Burkett's office to write some letters. A "Mr. MacKay" came in to see him, and he and Neighbors left to confer with Leeper, who was in a near-by building at the fort. Hardly had they departed when Burkett heard the report of a gun, and MacKay came hurrying back to

[14] 36 Cong., 1 sess., *Sen. Ex. Doc. 2*, I, 701.

his office, saying as he entered, "Major Neighbors is killed!" When Burkett rushed out of the building to look into the matter, he found Neighbors' body about fifty steps away.

"I directed the Sheriff to summon a jury to hold an inquest," Burkett wrote Mrs. Neighbors. "The jury assembled, witnesses were summoned to appear before me; and the jury, after hearing all the evidence, rendered its verdict that Major Robert S. Neighbors had come to his death by a shot from a double-barrel shotgun in the hands of Edward Cornett. . . .

"The body will be interred tomorrow morning, accompanied by the jury," he concluded. "I took from his person his gold watch, one pair of spectacles and case, $116 in money, one six-shooter and scabbard, one bowie knife and scabbard, one derringer pistol, one Sharps rifle, one silver pencil case, one pocketknife, one bunch of keys, one cartridge box and one overcoat. Frank Harris told me I had better hold them until I was directed where to send them."[15]

Camp Cooper was continued as a military post and expeditions were projected against hostile Comanches until the outbreak of the Civil War. In July, 1860, Major Thomas,[16] then in command of Camp Cooper, led a strong

[15] Robert S. Neighbors Papers, 1857–59.

[16] George H. Thomas was graduated from West Point on July 1, 1840, and commissioned as second lieutenant, Third Artillery. In later years he served gallantly in the Florida Seminole War, 1840–42; in Eastern and Western garrison duty, 1842–45; in the Mexican War, 1846–48; as instructor, West Point, 1851–54; on frontier duty in California, 1854–55; at Jefferson Barracks, Missouri, 1855. Then he came to Texas with the Second Cavalry and was closely associated with Lieutenant Colonel Robert E. Lee. Later, during the Civil War, he became a distinguished Northern commander, popularly known as the "Rock of Chickamauga," and rose to the rank of major general in the United States Army, December 15, 1864. Cullum, *Biographical Register,* I, 600–601.

force of the Second Cavalry in pursuit of a Comanche raiding party from a trail his scouts had picked up twenty-five miles east of Mountain Pass, a few miles south of present Merkel, Texas. The fleeing Indians were overtaken on the Salt Fork of the Brazos. They were so hard pressed that they abandoned their stolen horses and continued their flight. One of the warriors, however, lingered behind to cover their retreat, knowing, no doubt, that he would sacrifice his life by doing so. As the troopers closed in, with Thomas in advance, the Comanche kept up a rapid discharge of arrows, which wounded Thomas twice and wounded five of his enlisted men. Finally, the troopers killed the brave warrior, but not until his comrades had made their escape.

Another notable engagement with the Comanches occurred in December, 1860, when Captain L. S. Ross with a strong Texas Ranger force and aided by First Sergeant J. W. Spangler and a detachment of Company H, Second Cavalry, from Camp Cooper, surprised and destroyed a large Nokoni camp near the junction of Mule Creek and the Pease River, a few miles northeast of present-day Margaret, in northwestern Texas. In the fight Ross killed a warrior, mistakenly thought to be Peta Nocona, and one of his men overtook and captured an Indian woman, who with her baby was fleeing from camp. After the fight Ross and his men returned to Camp Cooper with their booty and prisoners.

Suspecting that the Nokoni female prisoner might be the long lost Cynthia Ann Parker, who had been taken as a child by the Comanches in 1836, Ross sent for Isaac Parker, her uncle. When Parker arrived, he interviewed the woman. She sat dejectedly on a box "with her chin on her hands and her elbows on her knees." When Parker could get no satisfactory replies to his questions from her, he turned to those standing near, saying that the captive was not Cynthia Ann, whereupon, with her face aglow with animation, she patted her breast, saying, "Cynthia Ann! Cynthia Ann!" James T. DeShields has said that "a ray of recollection sprang up in her mind that had been obliterated for twenty-five years."[17] After this reunion with her uncle, she returned with him to his Tarrant County home.

On February 18, 1861, Brevet Major General W. A. Twiggs, commanding the Department of Texas, agreed to surrender all the federal military posts in Texas to Texas troops. The actual surrender of Camp Cooper, however, was not effected until three days later, and then under very dramatic circumstances. At this time Captain S. D. Carpenter commanded the post with 250 men, which under ordinary circumstances would have been sufficient to defend it; therefore, when he observed the daily arrival of armed men on the hills on either side of the post and up and down the Clear Fork, he made hasty preparations for defense.

As soon as Carpenter learned that a part of the men surrounding Camp Cooper were Texas state troops, he inquired of their commander, Colonel W. C. Dalrymple, what his purpose was. Dalrymple answered that as commander of Texas troops he demanded the surrender of the post "with all arms, munitions, animals and other property heretofore belonging to the government of the U. S." Before surrendering, Carpenter informed Dalrymple that under ordinary circumstances his reply to such a demand would be "an

[17] James T. DeShields, *Border Wars of Texas* (Tioga, Texas, 1912), 184; Duke Parker to Carl Coke Rister, March 6, 1935.

unqualified refusal," but "in the present agitated political condition of our country I feel compelled to regard, in connection with this demand and its refusal, the perilous consequences that must result to the whole nation."[18] Consequently, on February 21, 1861, he acceded to Dalrymple's terms.

This regard for the nation's welfare or his unwillingness to defend his position, whatever his point of view might have been, evidently postponed the outbreak of the Civil War until April 12, 1861, when General P. G. T. Beauregard's guns began the conflict by firing on Fort Sumter.

When Captain Rogers, under Dalrymple's order, took possession of Camp Cooper, citizens who were present and had watched the transfer proceedings told Dalrymple that the doors of the different public storehouses "had been opened and the regular soldiery as well as other persons were permitted to take what they wanted to use or destroy, and that several tents with their contents comprising the quarters of a portion of the troops were burned as well as a good deal of other property, by the regular troops or others before their evacuation of the post, and that the doors of all public storehouses as well as officers' and mens' quarters were open and the whole post filled with persons when the State Troops entered the same."[19]

Dalrymple appointed Captain J. B. Barry to command the post and James H. Price of Erath County to be assistant quartermaster and commissary with a rank of lieutenant. Captain Barry stayed for only a few days and then left for other frontier duty.

[18] E. W. Winkler, ed., *Journal of the Secession Convention of Texas* (Austin, 1912), 386.
[19] *Ibid.*, 384.

Camp Cooper had offered a measure of practical training to officers who in later years were to rise to high rank in the Southern and Union armies. Among the notable Confederates were Robert E. Lee, William J. Hardee, Earl Van Dorn, E. Kirby Smith, and John B. Hood; and among the Union officers were George H. Thomas, I. N. Palmer, George Stoneman, and K. Garrard. What other frontier post could boast of such a brilliant galaxy of military stars?[20]

[20] Colonel M. L. Crimmins, "Camp Cooper and Fort Griffin," *West Texas Historical Association Year Book*, Vol. XVII (October, 1941), 38.

III A Troublous Interlude

IT IS SMALL wonder that Ketumse's Penatekas had agreed to forsake their nomadic life for sedentary security on the Clear Fork: their reservation was located in a beautiful valley, rich in natural resources. But the general area was seasonally inconstant; its encompassing hills, woodlands, and prairies could quickly change their spring and summer drabness when rain transformed them into vast fields of white daisies, yellow buttercups, and reddish-brown gaillardias. The Indians soon understood how necessary rain was in farming, for drought blighted the crops. Then the Indians began to long for the nomadic life again.

The keen-eyed ranchmen who rode up the Clear Fork Valley were not looking for flowers and beauty, although they were doubtless attracted by them. They were searching for unclaimed grasslands, and in this successful quest they became the spearhead of a new frontier advance.

Captain Newton C. Givens of the United States Second Dragoons had already pre-empted a choice seven-thousand-acre rangeland, five miles up the Clear Fork from Camp Cooper, before other cattlemen entered this ranchers' Eden.[1] In 1856, while Camp Cooper workmen were busy with hammer, saw, and trowel, substituting stone buildings for tents, Givens was designing an imposing ranch house on his near-by range land. Government freighters, who were hauling building materials and other supplies from San Antonio to Camp Cooper, were also accommodating him by delivering at his home site shingles, doors, and window sashes, at high freight charges.

And after a short time Givens' residence took shape. He had employed a mason to hew the stone and build the walls, and no doubt a carpenter to saw the lumber and put it in place. The new stone house was an imposing one, with two sixteen-by-twenty-foot rooms, divided by a twelve-foot hallway, with heavy doors leading into the hallway and from it into each room. In the east and west ends of the structure were chimneys providing each room with a wide, friendly fireplace. The walls were thick and the ceilings high, favoring a cool interior in summer and warmth in winter, for near at hand was an abundance of mesquite firewood.

A few yards west of this soon-to-be-named Old Stone Ranch was a smaller two-room stone building, with a single chimney rising from its center providing a fireplace for each room. This house may have been intended for a servant, or perhaps as a kitchen and dining room.[2]

A short distance southwest of the main ranch house was built a large stone corral with partition fences. Here at night calves and colts could be protected against the predatory lobos and panthers which abounded in the near-by timberland. A visitor who later inspected the corral

---

[1] Grant, "Early History of Shackelford County," as cited, 35–36.
[2] *Albany News,* December 25, 1931.

wrote humorously that the builder must have attempted to erect "a second Egyptian pyramid," for he had made the base of the corral only a little less than four feet thick and its walls five feet high, convexing at the top.[3]

Just south of his house, on the bank of Walnut Creek, Givens found a cool, pure spring, over which he built a rock springhouse; but in the hot summer, the spring ceased to run, and he dug a well, from which he drew water by means of a primitively fashioned sweep.

Fragmentary government records do not explain Givens' reasons for building the Old Stone Ranch. It is presumed that he brought his family there, for later occupants found near by the grave of a small child. Did he conceive it as a ranch house or a hunting lodge? The silent decades of almost a century do not supply the answer. If he intended to engage in ranching, he also spent much time in hunting. Near his home he could shoot buffalo, deer, and antelope; or, out on the prairie and the hills, he could find sport chasing coyotes, lobos, and panthers with his hounds.

But Givens' life at the old Stone Ranch was not entirely of unalloyed pleasure, for Indian Bureau records reveal that during his stay there he quarreled with the superintendent of the Texas Indians, Robert S. Neighbors.[4] Neighbors complained to General D. E. Twiggs that Givens, at the establishment of the agencies, had denounced the superintendent's "beef-eating" Indian policy and had said that no one but an army officer was fit to be an Indian

[3] *Ibid.*

[4] Leeper to Neighbors, March 29, 1858 (MS Division of War Records, A. G. O., National Archives, Washington); Neighbors to General D. E. Twiggs (MS Division of War Records, A. G. O., National Archives, Washington).

agent.[5] Neighbors also charged that Givens violated army regulations by owning and operating a cattle ranch, to which the doughty Captain replied that he had acquired no land on the Texas frontier, which no doubt was true. Indeed, few ranchers along the Texas border took the trouble to buy the land on which they ranged their cattle. Givens' fatal illness while in San Antonio on sick leave in 1859 ended the controversy.[6]

For a part of the time from 1859 to 1866 the Old Stone Ranch was the home of others, and at other times it stood lonely and deserted, well in advance of the "forted-up" frontier. Shortly after Givens' death, two men—a Mr. Knox and a Mr. Gardner—lived for a short time at the ranch house and ranged their cattle on the surrounding luxuriant grassland. But for some unknown reason they hastily departed, like the Arabs of yore who folded their tents and stole away, leaving buried near the house a variety of dishes and utensils.

The J. C. Lynches, the George Greers, the W. H. Ledbetters, and the Joe Matthewses were other early pioneers of the Clear Fork country who braved the vicissitudes and dangers of frontier life during the late 1850's or early 1860's. Lynch was a brash Irish youth who had come to the New World seeking adventure, and had found it in the California gold fields—had found, in fact, more than he had bargained for: hazardous living, tough companions, and dire want. Disappointed and disillusioned, he had then decided to go to Texas, whereupon in 1859 he joined an over-

[5] Neighbors to Twiggs, March 30, 1858 (MS in papers accompanying General D. E. Twiggs' Annual Report of the Department of Texas for 1858, A. G. O., Division of War Records, National Archives, Washington).
[6] Cullum, *Biographical Register*, I, 130.

land party of horseback riders to travel through southern Arizona and New Mexico.[7]

For many weary days, afflicted by heat, thirst, and hunger, these horsemen rode eastward. At last they reached El Paso, rested awhile, and again resumed their journey, this time into Texas. A short distance along the road, Lynch spied a deer two or three hundred yards away. He left his companions, rode as close to the unsuspecting animal as he could without arousing its fears, and then dismounted to steal closer for a good shot. Hidden near by was a party of marauding Indians, and when young Lynch had gone a short distance from his horse and was preparing to shoot his quarry, the Indians rode swiftly to his mount, untied it, and led it away, while its owner watched helplessly.

Lynch was bitterly disappointed. The Indians had stolen not only his horse and saddle, but also a pair of saddlebags filled with his extra clothing, his naturalization papers, which he had recently obtained in California, and other valuables. Yet the Indians had not seen fit to take his scalp, and for this he was grateful. Now on foot, he trudged back to the road and to his waiting companions, who had thought it best not to pursue the Indians.

After he and his comrades resumed their journey, they met a California-bound party consisting of Dr. Peter Gonsolus, his wife and lovely young daughter, hired men driving some cattle, and an irresponsible Dutchman who served as guide. Lynch had previously known the Dutchman at the gold diggings as an untrustworthy scoundrel, in whom Gonsolus should have placed no trust. When he voiced his opinion, the Dutchman heatedly denied his charges, and

[7] Don Biggers, *Shackelford County Sketches* (Albany, 1908). For this reference, see section of narrative carrying title "Early Settlers."

a quarrel followed, which ended in a fist fight. Lynch was the victor. Gonsolus then asked him to join his party for California. Lynch demurred, then hesitantly accepted, no doubt influenced more by his interest in Gonsolus' daughter than by any desire to return to the gold fields.

A short time later Lynch wooed and won the young lady. They were married in Santa Fé with Gonsolus' blessings, even though they had decided to return to Texas. A short time later they arrived in western Texas and located a ranch about six miles east of present Albany, on Hubbard Creek, a fine stream emptying into the Clear Fork.[8] During the trying Civil War years which followed, the young rancher and his wife proved that they had the stuff of which successful pioneers are made by running the gauntlet of border hardships, drought, and Indian dangers, and emerging as prominent community leaders.

Also among the first pioneers of the Hubbard Valley were George and Cal Greer, whose father had settled in 1860 in Shackelford County, about five miles up the Hubbard from Lynch's residence. Cal, William King, and Vol Simonds are credited with discovering the future site of the Ledbetter Salt Works.[9]

In 1861, these three men had driven a herd of cattle to the Concho River country, and on their return journey their horses had gotten away and left them afoot. Late in the afternoon the tired footmen made camp upon a small but clear creek.[10] They found that water in a spring near its

[8] Grant, "Early History of Shackelford County," as cited, 36–38; *Dallas Morning News*, July 8, 1934.

[9] Biggers, *Shackelford County Sketches.* See section title "Ledbetter Salt Works."

[10] This was the middle fork or Salt Fork of Hubbard Creek, eight miles southwest of present day Albany. See map accompanying James L.

bank was almost pure brine. When they finally reached home, they reported their discovery, and the settlers went to the spring with kettles to obtain a supply of much-needed salt.

The news of the discovery of a close-at-hand salt deposit was also carried to neighboring communities and counties, to Eastland, to Stephens, and to Throckmorton, whose settlers also came for salt. One of these was Billy McGough, who later wrote of his experience. "In 1862," he said, "we all got without salt. We had heard of a very salty place, to the northwest—a kind of spring where, in hot weather, you could rake up pure salt, except it was a little bitter.

"But bitter salt was better than no salt at all," as McGough said; and although the creek and spring were in Indian country, and, indeed, athwart a Comanche war trail to the white settlements, salt-hunting pioneers from homes fifty to sixty miles away came. McGough described the salt deposit as being in some of the roughest country of western Texas, lying between two mountains, on a prairie with very little timber of any kind. Indeed, timber was so sparse that McGough and others who sought to exaporate water from salt in kettles had to haul firewood for distances of ten miles or more. But here was precious salt, and they did not regard these long wood hauls as a serious handicap.

Eagerly, the pioneers dug shallow holes about the briny spring and creek, into which the water seeped. "We had carried along with us several pots, barrels, and kettles," McGough explained, "and by the time some of us got the wood with one wagon and three yoke of oxen, the rest of

Rock and W. I. Smith, *Southern and Western Texas Guide for 1878* (St. Louis, 1878). See also *Frontier Times*, Vol. XIX (July, 1942), 346.

the boys had ten or fifteen holes dug, which holes would soon run full of water. The water was salty as brine, but bitter and muddy, and it would not settle or get clear. So we would dig it up in our barrels. By the time it cooled in the barrels, it would be as clear as glass. Then we would pour it up into our kettles and boil it hard until salt began forming on the top, like ice. You could see it forming, and in a short time it would break and sink to the bottom of the kettle. . . . We made the prettiest and whitest salt I ever saw. After we got started it did not take us but a few days to make lots of salt."

A Comanche war party attacked others who came for salt. "They [the salt hunters] had hard luck," concluded McGough. "The Indians killed one of them and got their teams while they were out getting wood. I don't think they got much salt."[11]

In the next year McGough returned to the salt spring. He found that a stranger had pre-empted the site, had brought in huge iron kettles, and was manufacturing salt to sell, not only to the settlers but also to the Confederate government. The newcomer was W. H. Ledbetter, soon to become one of that frontier's most valuable citizens.

But Ledbetter's pre-emptive rights did not go unchallenged. Not long after he had established his salt works and had built his house, a Comanche war party appeared and offered battle. For several hours Ledbetter, his wife, and a hired hand withstood the Comanche attack, Mrs. Ledbetter reloading the guns of the two men as fast as they were fired and finally seizing a rifle and joining in the fray.[12] And at last the warriors withdrew, after they had suffered considerable loss in killed and wounded.

[11] Billy McGough Papers (MS, Hardin-Simmons University Library).

There were no public schools in the early sixties, so rancher Lynch hired a teacher, whose school was open to all the children of the neighborhood. And those children who lived a considerable distance from his ranch were invited to stay in his home.

The Ledbetters accepted Lynch's proposal and sent Johnnie to the ranch house. He soon became homesick, however, and late one evening slipped away from Lynch's and started toward home. As soon as his absence was noticed, the anxious cattleman organized searching parties and sent them out, but after fruitless days of looking for the lost child, they returned to the ranch.[13]

The lad's fate was never positively known, although nine years later a bronzed, unkempt young man drove into Fort Griffin to sell a wagonload of buffalo hides. He had come, he announced to inquisitive townsmen, from the Palo Duro Canyon of the Staked Plains. Local tradition has it that Ledbetter, after questioning the lad closely, announced that he was his long-lost son—truly a prodigal returned from Indian captivity. His captors had sold him, the lad stated, to a white renegade from the Palo Duro country, who had returned with him to his Staked Plains home. There the lad had been taught the white man's ways, even the rudiments of learning. Although the boy remained at Fort Griffin for a short time, it is said that he never consented to live with the Ledbetters and presently established a permanent residence in San Antonio, where he lived until his death.

Prior to this time the Ledbetters had exchanged their

[12] Edgar Rye, *The Quirt and the Spur: Vanishing Shadows of the Texas Frontier* (Chicago, 1909), 117–18.
[13] *Ibid.*, 121ff.

beyond-the-frontier Salt Fork residence for a new picket house (covered with buffalo hides) on the Clear Fork, a short distance from the future site of Fort Griffin, where they were living when the young stranger came to the Flat.[14]

"Uncle Joe" Matthews and John and Bill Hittson were other notable cattlemen who settled in the Clear Fork country, the latter two moving into one of the officers' buildings at Camp Cooper.[15] "Uncle Joe" established his residence two miles down the river below where Fort Griffin was later built.[16] He also became a substantial citizen of the Clear Fork country, and led in a movement for law and order.

John and Bill Hittson did not move out to the Camp Cooper area until 1866, but while they were at Fort Davis their deeds of heroism in fighting Indian raiders had become legendary. On one occasion, while scouting, they were attacked by a strong Comanche war party on Tecumseh Creek east of Fort Davis. While the two men were keeping the Indians at bay, a Negro companion went for help. Meanwhile, during the early part of the fight, Bill was wounded and John dragged him under an overhanging rock of a creek bluff for protection until help should arrive. John inflicted such deadly execution on his attackers, however, that presently they rode away with their wounded, leaving three dead warriors behind.

[14] Grant, "Early History of Shackelford County," as cited, 44.

[15] "Frontier Life of John Chadbourne Irwin" in J. R. Webb Papers (MS, R. N. Richardson Collection, Hardin-Simmons University Library).

[16] *Ibid.*, 39; Ben O. Grant, "Explorers and Early Settlers of Shackelford County," *West Texas Historical Association Year Book*, Vol. XI (November, 1935), 32.

A Troublous Interlude

The Civil War years had wrought radical changes along the Texas frontier. Both Union and Confederate troops had been employed for active service either within the state or on eastern war fronts. Only Confederate token guards had been left at border posts, and at Phantom Hill and Camp Cooper even these were presently withdrawn and the region was left without defenders, except those men who had "forted-up" or who settled together for mutual protection at Old Picketsville, Fort Davis, Owl's Head, Lynch's ranch, or elsewhere. This "forting-up" movement, however, was caused by a devastating Indian raid.

In October, 1864, about two hundred Kiowa and Comanche raiders, led by Little Buffalo, bedecked in war paint, feathers, and gaudy trappings, rode across Red River to attack the border settlements sixty miles south of present-day Wichita Falls. They fell upon a Confederate outpost, "Fort" Murrah, in Young County, about twelve miles west of Fort Belknap, killed five of its troopers, and chased back into the "fort" fifteen others who came out to meet them.[17] Then they devastated the Elm Creek settlement, killing Joel Meyers, Dr. T. J. Wilson, and James McCoy and his son Miles, and carried away into captivity the Widow Patrick, her two granddaughters, the two Durgan sisters, and the wife and children of Britt Johnson, a former Negro orderly at Fort Belknap. Captain W. S. Nye states that in 1865 Britt visited the friendly Penateka camp of

[17] J. W. Wilbarger, *Indian Depredations in Texas* (Austin, 1889), 58off. Wilbarger states that fifteen Texas Rangers were driven back into the fort, but Captain Buck Barry later wrote that it was a company of Colonel James Bourland's regiment which was repulsed. See James K. Greer, ed., *A Texas Ranger and Frontiersman: The Days of Buck Barry in Texas, 1805–1906* (Dallas, 1932), 180.

Asa-Havey and through his help exchanged horses for the captives, including his own family.[18]

Sam Newcomb, a former county clerk and surveyor of Stephens County, kept a diary in which is found an interesting record of "Fort Davis" life. This "fort," wrote Newcomb, was on the east bank of the Clear Fork, about fifteen miles below Camp Cooper. About 125 people—men, women, and children—had sought its protection from the Indians.[19] Here was a tightly knit community occupying a space of 600 by 375 feet and divided into sixteen lots. Each lot was 75 feet square, and a 25-foot alley ran through the village from east to west. Here, Newcomb wrote, were built "twenty good houses. . . . That is, good houses of the kind. They were built with pickets, covered with dirt, and while not very ornamental, they are very comfortable."[20]

[18] W. S. Nye, *Carbine and Lance* (Norman, 1937), 46. Wilbarger, *Indian Depredations in Texas,* 58off., has a different Britt Johnson story. Wilbarger states that Britt traveled alone onto the Staked Plains, made friends with the Quahadas, and during the summer of 1865 succeeded in mounting the captives on horses and escaping with them. Millie Durgan was never recovered. She was adopted by a noted Kiowa warrior of the Ko-eet-senko clan and spent the remainder of her life among the Kiowas.

[19] "Frontier Life of John Chadbourne Irwin," as cited. John Irwin states: "As I remember there were about 25 families forted up there during the war. . . . John Selman and his mother . . . Uncle Henry Anderson, old man Musgraves and family, Tom and Arch Ratliff and the January family . . . the Anderson family and Edgar Christenson . . . Uncle Watt Reynolds and family . . . the Boswells . . . and a family named Steele and next to them lived Jim Thorpe . . . then J. M. Frans, the keeper of the Butterfield station at the Indian reservation before the war . . . Sam Newcomb, the school teachers, and T. E. Jackson and family about completed the list." See also Grant, "Explorers and Early Settlers of Shackelford County," *West Texas Historical Association Year Book,* Vol. XI (November, 1935), 27.

[20] Marilynne Howsley, "Forting Up on the Texas Frontier during the Civil War," *West Texas Historical Association Year Book,* Vol. XVII (October, 1941), 71ff.; Sam Newcomb's diary, entry of January 1, 1865.

Those men who were permitted by law to be left at this border post were under frontier service regulations; that is, for one-fourth of their stay at home they were required to drill and to patrol the border; for the remaining three-fourths of their time they could attend to their own affairs. And under no circumstances could they be required to remain away from home more than two months at a time.

At best, life on the Texas border was hazardous and exacting. Whenever they had the advantage, Indian pillagers stole the settlers' horses, drove away hundreds of cattle, and attacked scouting parties. More than once, men of Fort Davis out in search of livestock were chased back to the post by Indians who stopped only when they came into the clearing of the settlement. Then, when the Fort Davis men quickly organized a force to go in pursuit, almost uniformly the Indians, mounted on swift horses, could keep out of harm's way.

Still, life at Fort Davis must go on. Often a wagon train was sent over a rough road to Weatherford for meal, salt, and other supplies. Newcomb's diary stressed the importance of such supplies. An entry of January 31, 1865, ran, "The crowd that left here before Christmas for breadstuff returned this evening. They came in good time as there were not many rations of flour or meal in the fort when they arrived." But the "forted-up" families could live without bread, as there was an abundance of good beef and pecans. In addition, the Clear Fork and its affluents abounded in fish; Fort Davis hunters could kill turkeys, prairie chicken, quail, antelope, deer, and bison in the surrounding country.

Fort Davis women proved their resourcefulness and mettle in every crisis. They were too far from the nearest market to make such periodic purchases as much-needed clothing, food, and medicines. But undaunted, again and again they proved that necessity is the mother of invention. They changed deerskin into soft, pliable buckskin, from which they made trousers, moccasins, and gloves; they made hair nets—gray, black, or brown—from horse hair to satisfy each woman's preference; and when wool was available, they spun thread, wove cloth, and cut and sewed it into garments for all. They made their own candles, and soap and soda from lye leached from wood ashes. When their family or neighbors were sick, they concocted medicinal brews from herbs; when physicians could not be called, they served as midwives, although occasionally, when a patient's life depended on a doctor's skill, a settler must ride a hundred miles or more for him. Labor, hardship, and ever present danger of Indian attack were the frontier women's daily lot. That they made easier and more endurable the lives of those they loved and that they helped to develop a virile and thrifty border life is tribute enough.

Only a small minority of those who "forted-up" were border toughs and ne'er-do-wells. Most of the residents were law-abiding, responsible people, who sought to improve themselves. Sam Newcomb's subscription school, for example, was well attended, not only by small children, but also by young men and women. In fact, as Newcomb's diary reveals, occasionally a young couple quit school to marry.

A Sunday school was also organized at the home of J. A. Frans, although the only suitable literature available was the Bible. The earnest students would listen to one of their number read a comforting passage, and all would discuss it, after which old and young would engage in a spelling bee from Webster's *Blue Back Speller.*

The humdrum of Fort Davis life was mitigated occasionally by bison invasions or by the appearance of the dreaded Indian raiders.[21] Once Professor Newcomb, the Connecticut school teacher, entered in his diary: "Cold and sleeting. Several herds of buffaloes drifted by during the day. I have stood in the school house and watched a herd not more than 100 yards away. What a show this would be in my native state where there is not wild game larger than a fox; but game of all kinds, even wild hogs and horses, is plentiful here."[22]

Newcomb could not watch with as complete detachment the Comanches who might appear, for they were after white scalps and captives as well as horses. On a blustery March day, he wrote that excitement was high, that about nine o'clock that morning, "Mr. McCarthy came upon a large body of Indians" who chased him back into the fort. Quickly, the settlers rode out in retaliation, but the Indians turned and fled and were not overtaken. The Comanches' boldness in riding directly up to the settlement must have alarmed the settlers greatly, for Newcomb concluded, "I think this will stir some people in this place to do their share of picketing." Undoubtedly he remembered his own experience with Comanche war parties while sur-

[21] Both Sam Newcomb and his wife, Susan, kept diaries in which are found their day-to-day experiences. Each diary is arranged in two parts. Sam's account was divided into the periods, January 1 to December 21, 1865, and January 1 to August 1, 1866; Susan's from August 1, 1865 to December 14, 1869, and from January 1, 1871, to June 4, 1873. Only Sam's diary was published in part in Biggers, *Shackelford County Sketches.* Mrs. Ed Dodge of Albany, Texas, permitted the author to use her bound typewritten copies of the Newcomb diaries. The present location of the original documents is not known.

[22] Sam Newcomb's diary; Mrs. Sallie Reynolds Matthews, *Interwoven* (Houston, 1936), 25.

veying the Stephens County boundary line, for more than once he had escaped from them only because he was mounted on a faster horse.

On one occasion Comanche warriors were uninvited guests at a Fort Davis dance, and probably had sardonic pleasure in dancing to the white fiddler's music. Young settlers had ridden in from communities farther east, and when the dance ended just before dawn, they came out for their horses, only to find them gone—the Indians had stolen them. Next morning, when the settlers sought the marauders' trail, they picked it up directly under the window of the home in which the dance was held. There in the soft earth were the tell-tale moccasin tracks of the Indians, who had danced in a circle to the fiddler's music before they had taken the white men's horses.[23]

The Fort Davis young men and women eagerly looked forward to every occasion for entertainment—dances, play parties, picnics, horseback riding, marriages, and all kinds of public occasions—for border life at its best was lonely. Fiddlers volunteered to furnish music for the dances, for generally young gallants present would pass the hat to collect for them the appreciative dancers' nickels and dimes. Candy pullings were also enjoyed, when the candy was made from molasses, usually heavy "sarghum," cooked in the family washpot. But a community wedding of a popular young man and woman was the highlight of the season. For days before such an occasion, a fond mother, mother-in-law, or aunt made ready an "infare," assisted by a neighbor's wife, by days of roasting and baking meats, pies, and

[23] J. R. Webb, "Chapters from the Frontier Life of Phin W. Reynolds," *West Texas Historical Association Year Book*, Vol. XXI (October, 1945), 117; Matthews, *Interwoven*, 28.

Courtesy Colorado Historical Museum

General Philip Henry Sheridan

cakes. The wedding party was feasted bountifully, enjoyed an all-night dance and, throughout the night, plenty of coffee and cake.

A death or some other tragedy reminded the settlers of life's frailty. At best Fort Davis life was raw. There were even days when the settlers had little or nothing to eat, when it was difficult for them to keep the cold winter wind from whistling through the cracks of their crudely built picket houses. And death or prolonged illness, because of lack of proper medical attention, was a common experience.

At last, in May, 1865, darkness gave way to light; Fort Davis residents learned that the Civil War was over.[24] Veterans, in increasing numbers, tired and spiritless, came back to the Clear Fork frontier. The settlers accepted the South's defeat, and began the work of reconstruction. With the return of their own men there was now no need for civilian forts, and Fort Davis families in ones and twos sought new homes. Several families moved up the Clear Fork to Camp Cooper, where the last soldiers stationed there had left some partly furnished houses. Others turned eastward to Stephens County, or farther east to settlements comparatively free from Indian raids.

Poverty yet stalked the land and business opportunities were few. Fortunately, border cattlemen could range their cattle on vast unoccupied free grasslands. The Civil War had inured them to hardships and deprivations, and had caused them to believe that luxuries, and even clothing and food, could be had only by hard work.

About the middle of October, 1865, records Mrs. Sallie Reynolds Matthews,[25] her brother George, Si Hough, and

[24] Matthews, *Interwoven*, 28; Susan Newcomb's diary.
[25] *Interwoven*, 30; Susan Newcomb's diary.

Riley St. John drove a small herd of steers to New Mexico—
the first postwar herd driven from Texas to New Mexico.
They feared Indian trouble, but completed their dangerous
drive without serious mishap, although they did have narrow escapes. They had bought their cattle in the Clear
Fork country for eight or ten dollars a head and sold them
for sixty dollars, making a profit of fifty dollars a head.
George and Si returned to Fort Davis on January 16, 1866.
Riley had left them in New Mexico to go to Denver to
receive his share of a mining property which his partner
had recently sold.

Shortly after the cattlemen returned home, the B. W.
Reynolds family—the father and mother, the children, Sam
Newcomb, a son-in-law, and a grandson—moved out to the
Old Stone Ranch. Si Hough, Flake Barber, Levi Shaw, and
Mart Hoover went with them. "We had a retinue of eight
grown men," wrote Mrs. Matthews, "three boys ranging
in age from fourteen down to eight years, two women, one
little girl and a baby boy, for [at Fort Davis] on August 21,
1865, there had been born into my sister's home a little son,
Samuel August Newcomb, always called 'Gus,' the first
grandchild in the family."[26]

The place was just as its former occupants had left it.
One of the two main rooms had been floored with plank,
but the other one and the hallway were of flagstone. On
one side of this stone-floored room Mother Reynolds' bed
was placed, and on the other a lengthy dining table for
fifteen, counting those who came with the family. The new
occupants were fortunate in finding a few pieces of furniture in the two rooms—chairs and a French bedroom suite
decorated with a spray of flowers on the head and foot

[26] *Interwoven,* 33.

50

boards of the bed and on the dresser drawers. To the Reynolds women, who had just come from Fort Davis' squalor and drabness, this suite was the symbol of elegance.

The newcomers liked the Old Stone Ranch. South of the house and beyond a grassy prairie, mesquite flats interspersed the open country, and northeast of it, about half a mile distant, was a small butte, which Susan Newcomb called "Buzzard Peak,"[27] so well described in her diary. Here, late in the evenings, she sometimes maintained an anxious watch for the return of her husband and brothers, when they had been away hunting cattle, or perhaps on an Indian scout. West of the ranch house was Indian country. From Buzzard's Peak one could see in the distance the green-tree meanderings of Paint Creek and the Clear Fork, and the wild panorama of virgin hills, meadows, and forests. There was no other trace of a white man's habitation between the Old Stone Ranch and the eastern settlements of New Mexico, several hundred miles away.

The Reynoldses were treated to an agreeable surprise a short time after they had moved into their new home. One day while Glenn was digging in a rock pile a short distance from the house, he found a large wooden box of dishes which Knox and Gardner had buried there before leaving. Now Mrs. Reynolds had enough dishes and plates for her large family and did not have to supplement her limited chinaware pieces with tin plates, as she had previously done.

This discovery led to other searches for hidden treasures in every stone-littered mound about the ranch. Among other things, the diggers found cowbells and staples for

[27] Both Mrs. Matthews and Susan Newcomb give space in their accounts to this family lookout station.

ox-yokes, for all of which Reynolds paid the former owners when they again visited the ranch. In one mound, a tiny baby's coffin was found, which they immediately recovered. It is not known who the infant's parents were, but probably the Givenses.[28]

The Old Stone Ranch stood in the center of a hunter's paradise. At all times thousands of buffalo grazed the open country about the house in small herds of fifties and hundreds, but closely bunched together; farther west, back in the hills, were herds of antelope, deer, and wild horses. Glenn and Phin caught buffalo calves and kept them in the stone corral, and the men hung buffalo tongues and humps in the smokehouse, as well as choice parts of antelope and deer.

Susan Newcomb's day-by-day diary is filled with accounts of hunting trips. One such instance is her entry of January 7, 1867: "The men all went hunting today. Sam, Si, Ben, and Uncle Matt Frans went together. . . . An hour or two by sun, Uncle Matt and Ben came in tired and hungry. They had killed one buffalo and came after a horse to bring in the hide and tallow. In a little while Sam and Si came in. Sam had pulled off his overshirt and filled the sleeves full of tallow, tied the ends together and swung it over his shoulder like a shot pouch. About sunset William and Levi got in with four tongues and a deer. After dark Elizie and Dock came in; they had killed fourteen buffalo and three deer."

From the timber along the Clear Fork and Walnut Creek the household was supplied in winter with bushels of pecans and walnuts and with fat turkey gobblers. During crisp fall and winter evenings, the family sat about a

[28] Matthews, *Interwoven*, 36.

log fire, the boys molding bullets from bar lead, and their mother and sisters sewing, knitting, and mending— all with faces aglow and appetites whetted by the aroma of roasting pecans and buffalo tongues buried in the hot ashes.

An occasional camp-out on the Clear Fork added variety to their experiences. Susan described such a diversion. Keenly aware of the tedious life his stay-at-home family led while he and the older boys were out looking for cattle or scouting, on October 22, 1866, rancher Reynolds loaded his ox-drawn wagon with cooking utensils, food, and bedding, and, together with his wife and children, traveled westward a few miles to a point where the old California Trail crossed Paint Creek. They forded the Clear Fork a short distance below the junction of the two streams, established a camp, and spent two days gathering a winter's supply of pecans, wild turkeys, venison, and even ripe prickly-pear apples.

But the vagaries of the weather marred their outing. On the afternoon of the third day dark clouds hid the sun. After hours of delay, caused by a search for strayed oxen, at last they found and yoked them to the wagon, and pulled out from camp, homeward-bound. It was necessary for them to ford the Clear Fork before swollen waters kept them from doing so. By the time they had reached the crossing, rain was falling, and the driver whipped his slow-moving oxen down into the river bed, while the muddy water swirled about them.

But when the wagon was in midstream, the oxen broke loose and ran up the opposite bank, leaving the panic-stricken family stranded. The boys climbed from the wagon into the river, waded ashore, caught the oxen, recoupled them, and made a new start for the east bank. Again the now frightened oxen broke away and fled up the opposite bank, and again they were caught, brought back into the rising water, and a successful crossing was finally made. The oxen were wild with fright. The wagon wheels were scotched, and the oxen were allowed to tug and run, the family no doubt enjoying their labors in doing so.[29]

Susan did not write about the ever present Indian danger while she and her family were far within their country, although she must always have been aware of it. Indian raids had not ceased with the end of the Civil War, for many stressful months were yet to elapse before federal troops came to man the border posts. Consequently, the Reynoldses experienced the dread realism of Indian warfare when they had hardly acclimated themselves.

During the summer following their arrival at this exposed ranch house, Reynolds, accompanied by his son Ben, Mrs. Susan Newcomb and her baby Gus, and Sallie, made his yearly trip to Weatherford for supplies. Mrs. Newcomb and Sallie had gone with him to visit relatives, the Barbers, and to have their pictures (tintypes) made.

On the Sunday following their departure, a painted and feathered party of fourteen warriors swooped down on the ranch. Most of the men were away at that time, having left only two older men as guards and the two youngest boys, Glenn and Phin. The painted raiders, adorned in war bonnets and other trappings, whooping and firing their guns, rode recklessly up to the ranch house, dismounted at the corral, let out the penned buffalo calves, and rounded up and drove away more than three hundred cattle. This act, indeed, was unusual for Comanche raiders, for they

[29] Susan Newcomb's diary gives an extended account of this picnic, including her entries of October 22, 23, and 24, 1866.

seldom bothered with cattle; generally they came for horses. It may have been, as the Clear Fork pioneers frequently said, that they were white outlaws dressed as Indians. Glenn joined the two men in firing at the raiders, who beat a hasty retreat.[30]

A second Indian scare came in April, 1867. The Indians raided farther down the Clear Fork, and this time drove away some horses. Settlers rode in hot haste to the Old Stone Ranch for help, and George and Will Reynolds and Si Hough joined them in pursuit. The settlers, thus strengthened, followed the well-marked trail for about forty miles and at last overtook the Indians on the Double Mountain Fork of the Brazos, in western Haskell County.[31]

The Indians, believing that they were safe from pursuit, had made camp and were taking their ease, some hunting buffalo, when their pursuers appeared. As the vengeful party galloped up, the Indians took to their horses and scattered like quail, but to no avail. With a yell, the white men charged, shooting right and left. As Indian after Indian fell in the running fight, the settlers stopped long enough to collect scalps and accoutrements of war. But they also suffered casualties—John Anderson was shot through the arm, and, while George Reynolds and Si Hough were close in pursuit, the chief of the raiding party, armed with bow and arrow, shot George from his horse. The arrow struck a large belt buckle George was wearing and was de-

[30] *Albany News,* December 25, 1931; Matthews, *Interwoven,* 39; Susan Newcomb's diary.

[31] Although both Mrs. Matthews and Susan Newcomb wrote interesting accounts of this Indian raid and defeat, readable recent narratives are found in Webb, "Chapters from the Frontier Life of Phin W. Reynolds," *West Texas Historical Association Year Book,* Vol. XXI (October, 1945), 120–21; *The Fort Worth Press,* September 19, 1953.

flected, entering his body just above the navel and lodging in the muscular part of his back. George quickly pulled the shaft from his body, but without the arrowhead.

When Si hastened up and saw his friend on the ground, apparently dying, he vowed that he would have the scalp of the warrior who shot him. The chief was not hard to find, for he wore gay trappings and a bonnet of eagle feathers and the bridle of his horse was ornamented by hammered silver disks. True to his vow, Si overtook the chief, shot him from his horse, dismounted, ripped his scalp from his head, and took it away as a bloody trophy. Only one of the warriors was allowed to escape.[32]

Meanwhile, the white victors were in a quandary. They were far from the Old Stone Ranch, the nearest habitation. George was desperately wounded. They had no medical supplies and knew nothing about meeting such an emergency. What should they do?

At least they could notify George's family at the Old Stone Ranch, and two of their number, William and George Anderson, rode posthaste on this mission. Those left behind rigged up an often-used border expedient, a pack-stretcher, although they were doubtful that they could return the suffering man to his family. Then they tied two horses together, neck and tail, and fastened securely between them their "kayak," or pack-stretcher, and placed their blankets on it. Then they lifted the wounded man onto this new device and slowly started their homeward journey.

Two men rode guard on either side of the horse-carriers, and another in front. Thus hour after hour they moved

[32] Matthews, *Interwoven*, 40ff.; *Albany News*, December 25, 1931; *The Fort Worth Press*, September 19, 1953.

ahead. At last the wounded man's journey of agony neared an end. They came in view of the ranch house, where Glenn and Phin kept watch from atop the smokehouse. When they had counted the full number of those who had left on horses, they quickly relayed the glad news to the anxious family, for they had expected George to die of his wound. As the returning party neared the ranch house, the brave man had persuaded his comrades to put him on his horse so that he could allay the fears of those who would be on watch.

Meanwhile, Sam Newcomb had ridden night and day for a doctor from Weatherford, one hundred miles away, stopping only long enough to get food and to change mounts at ranches along the way. With no rest, he and Dr. James D. Ray rode just as hastily and unceasingly on the return trip.

When they reached the Old Stone Ranch, Dr. Ray found that he could do little for the wounded man. He had brought with him neither surgical instruments nor anesthetics; he probed the wound, shook his head, and did little more. Surprisingly enough, the spike imbedded in George's body caused no infection, and after many days, the wound healed, although it caused him much suffering in later years, until in the summer of 1882, George went to Kansas City and had the spike removed. The *Kansas City Journal*, of July 18 of that year, reported the successful operation. "Yesterday afternoon," the report read, "there was removed from the body of George T. Reynolds, a prominent cattleman of Fort Griffin, Texas, an arrowhead, 2 inches long. Reynolds had carried this head 16 years, 3 months, and 15 days.

"On Friday last, the gentleman came to this city and

registered at the St. James Hotel. His coming was for the purpose of having a surgical operation."

No anesthetic was used. George had exacted a promise from the surgeon that if he should ask him to halt the operation, he would do so. Two of George's friends accompanied him into the operating room, but one of them sickened and left hastily. The other, Shanghai Pierce, a well-known South Texas cattleman, is reported to have shouted as the surgeon's knife deepened the incision: "Stop, Doctor! You are cutting that man to the hollow!" Whereupon George called a halt, sat up on the operating table, and the arrowhead, which had eluded the knife, slipped from the incision.

Later in the summer of 1867 the Reynolds family was in for another ripple of excitement. Across the valley south of the Old Stone Ranch came riding a large number of men who the family at first thought were Indians. "Everyone hastily gathered into the house," wrote Mrs. Matthews later, "and guns were looked to as men made ready for defense. . . . Soon, however, they could see bayonets glistening in the sun, and, as they came nearer, the blue coats and brass buttons of a detachment of United States cavalry looked beautiful indeed to this Old Stone Ranch family. They were most welcome guests from the outside world. They were a part of the Sixth Cavalry that had been sent out by the government to establish another fort for the protection of the Texas frontier."[33]

[33] *Interwoven*, 50. On August 4, following, Mrs. Susan Newcomb heard the early morning bugle call at the Sixth Cavalry camp on Uncle Matt Frans' Clear Fork Ranch. One soldier was wearing "iron hopples," she said.

IV Fort Griffin, Border Guardian

J UST AS THE lack of military protection had been the
weakness of the Texas frontier during the Civil War,
now the reactivation and building of army posts in advance
of the border's "cutting edge" became its strength. Once
again the federal government assumed its burden of pro-
tecting the frontier under its joint-resolution agreement
with Texas in 1845.

When with the dawn of peace in 1865 those settlers
who had "forted-up" at Fort Davis, Picketville, and elsewhere along the frontier began to leave their posts to seek
new homes, some traveled eastward to areas far removed
from the border, while others braved Indian dangers and became the vanguards of postwar settlement. But the nomadic
Comanches and Kiowas neither were parties to the recent
Confederate surrender agreements nor were they ready for
peace. For more than a decade, in fact, they had watched
with growing resentment settler encroachments on their
choice hunting ranges. Soon their game would be destroyed
and their lands occupied by the advancing white man unless they stopped him.[1]

[1] Agent William Bent had thus voiced Comanche and Kiowa con-

These Indians had been accustomed to a free, open life, to hunting the buffalo and pitching their lodges anywhere between the Arkansas and the Río Grande. This was the land for which they had fought and which they had won. Both the Apaches and the Spaniards had receded before their advance, and since the latter part of the eighteenth century they had been the lords of the South Plains.[2]

So now the nomads had a hard choice to make. Either they must drive the white man out of their country or they must submit to him and surrender their ancient customs and life. They chose the former course, which meant a war to the finish.

During the Civil War period, again and again the Comanches and Kiowas, in large and small war parties, had slipped across Red River to raid the Texas border, to burn, kill, and steal. Border homes were left in ashes, fields were in grass and weeds, fences were down, livestock had been driven away, and widespread desolation had supplanted orderly settlement.

So bold had been the Indians' "system of murder and robbery," observed an army visitor, "that since June, 1862, not less than 800 persons [up to 1868] have been murdered, —the Indians escaping from the troops by travelling at night when their trail could not be followed, thus giving enough distance and time to render pursuit, in most cases, fruitless."[3] These statements were borne out by another ob-

cern. See *Annual Report of the Commissioner of Indian Affairs, 1850* (Washington, 1851), 137–39.

[2] For excellent discussions of the Indians' point of view, see Richardson, *The Comanche Barrier,* 291ff.; Ernest Wallace and E. Adamson Hoebel, *The Comanches: Lords of the South Plains* (Norman, 1952), 306ff.

server, who wrote, in 1866, that the whole of the state's frontier line of counties, west of Grayson County, had been subject to the inroads of the Indians for the past four years and that the population of Jack County was only about one-fourth of what it had been. The border counties had been deserted, owing to increased Indian dangers, while able-bodied settlers were away with the Confederate armies.[4]

The *Waco Register* reported on April 21, 1866, that the Indians—mostly Comanches—swarmed all through the country—and that not more than one-fifth of the old ranches were occupied. A great many people had left and others were leaving, and the whole country was in a desperate condition. The writer seems not to have known that the buffalo range then extended east of Camp Cooper and Phantom Hill, a fact which may have accounted for the presence of some of the Indians.

There is abundant proof that white outlaws were in league with Comanche and Kiowa raiders. Professor W. C. Holden, for instance, found in the papers of the Texas Adjutant General's Office an interesting letter which hints at the illicit traffic conducted by outlaw gangs across Red River and of the contact between certain Indians and whites. The letter, taken from the body of an Indian raider killed by Second Cavalry troopers from Camp Cooper, was written by an outlaw at "Caddew [Caddo] Creek" to his "Dear Chum" in Texas. The letter explained that "Page, our faithful guide" would be bringing the letter since he

[3] P. H. Sheridan (comp.), *Records of Engagements with Hostile Indians within the Military Division of the Missouri, 1862–1882* (Washington, 1882), 16.

[4] *Circular No. 4*, S. G. O. (Washington, December 5, 1870); *Flake's Daily Bulletin* (Galveston), April 27, 1866, observed that Indian raiding had reached within the vicinity of Austin, the Texas capital.

was going to Texas anyway to settle a small matter "with a couple of fellows on the Clear Fork." This undelivered message indicates that such Indians as Page co-operated with white outlaws in driving stolen horses across Red River and co-operated, no doubt, in other acts of thievery and depredation.[5]

Thomas C. Battey, a Quaker schoolteacher among the wild Kiowas, had more complete evidence of white-outlaw culpability. In the early 1870's he wrote that white thieves from Texas had made a raid into Indian Territory and had stolen "about two hundred head of ponies and mules from Indian herds." He later added that a North Texas sheriff had told him that "twice in his official capacity he had called out a portion of the militia to put down depredators in his county, and in the ensuing skirmishes . . . two had been killed. The individuals killed on both occasions proved to be white men, so thoroughly disguised with false hair, masks, and Indian equipage, as to readily be mistaken for Indians."[6]

The settlers were impatient because the War Department was slow to send cavalry and infantry to protect their interests. The sinuous Texas border line extended thirteen hundred miles from the Red River to the Río Grande, on every part of which the settlements had been, and still were exposed to Indian and white outlaw raids.

After a landslide of angry letters, petitions, and memorials from the border had poured into Congress and the offices of responsible military authorities, at last the commander of the Department of Texas was ordered to re-

[5] Richardson, *The Comanche Barrier*, 250n.
[6] Thomas C. Battey, *A Quaker among the Indians* (Boston, 1875), 206, 239n.

establish a frontier line of defense. The old line, from south
to north, had included Forts Duncan, Clark, Territt, Mc-
Kavett, Chadbourne, and Phantom Hill, and the supply
post of Preston on Red River. This line was now modified
and, at points, advanced. Fort Richardson, near Jacksboro,
was built to protect Texas counties immediately south of
Red River. Then other posts farther south, Griffin, the subposts of Belknap, Phantom Hill, and Chadbourne, and
Forts Concho[7] and McKavett were either reactivated or
built.[8] From Fort McKavett, two lines of military posts
were projected: one into the Big Bend country, composing
Forts Stockton, Davis, Quitman, and Bliss; the other following down the Río Grande, consisting of Forts Clark,
Duncan, McIntosh, and Brown.[9]

Lieutenant Colonel S. D. Sturgis[10] was disturbed by
the rumor that Fort Belknap was to become a permanent
post in spite of its alarming defense inadequacies. He had

[7] The important role which the border post played in frontier defense is well presented in J. Evetts Haley, *Fort Concho and the Texas
Frontier* (San Angelo, 1952).

[8] A small guard was also kept by Fort Griffin troopers (stationed at
Phantom Hill) at the Mountain Pass mail station, about fifty miles southwest of Fort Griffin.

[9] A manuscript map showing these posts and the general line of
defense is included with the Texas departmental commander's "Annual
Report of 1869" (File No. 1538–M, A. G. O., War Records, National
Archives, Washington). See also Carl Coke Rister, *The Southwestern
Frontier, 1865–1881* (Cleveland, 1928), 48ff.

[10] After Sturgis had graduated from West Point, he was assigned to
the Second Dragoons as a brevet second lieutenant. He was with the
Dragoons during the Mexican War. Then, still as a Dragoon officer, he
served on the California frontier, 1848–51; in Kansas, 1851–52; in New
Mexico, 1852–55; and in Kansas and Indian Territory, 1855–61. During
the Civil War he served on both the Eastern and Western fronts, taking
part in such hard-fought engagements as the Seven Days' Battle and
Fredericksburg. Cullum, *Biographical Register,* II, 159–60.

also heard that four thousand Arapaho, Cheyenne, and Comanche warriors were on the warpath five days' march from Belknap. Were they to descend on him, he could not offer successful resistance. Consequently, he dispatched Lieutenant H. B. Mellen up the Clear Fork to look for a better site for a post. Mellen was presently back, reporting on an easily defensible site on a hill overlooking the Clear Fork, thirty-five miles away. Sturgis accepted Mellen's report and sent him hurrying to Galveston to have the commanding general approve it. The result was the establishment of Fort Griffin at the site he had chosen.

At Belknap, not even the horses and mules would drink from the saline Brazos. A post well had been dug, but it furnished little water. Then, as a temporary expedient, water wagons had been sent to Elm Creek, six miles away, but they could not supply enough water for such a large post. At Fort Griffin, Sturgis found that by establishing short water-hauls from Collins Creek and the Clear Fork and supplementing the supply with a post well, his problem was solved.

The Clear Fork frontiersmen were pleased to learn on the afternoon of July 31, 1867, that Lieutenant Colonel S. D. Sturgis had led a considerable cavalry force from Fort Belknap to the Clear Fork to establish there an important military post. His command was an all-cavalry unit—four companies of the Sixth Cavalry (F, I, K, and L). It was not until June 3 of the next year that companies of the Seventeenth Infantry, under Lieutenant Colonel S. B. Hayman,[11] were added to the garrison.

[11] *Ibid.*, II, 68. Hayman, who succeeded Sturgis as commandant of Fort Griffin, also had previous border service in Wisconsin, New Mexico, and Texas. He was also a Mexican War veteran, and fought in the battles

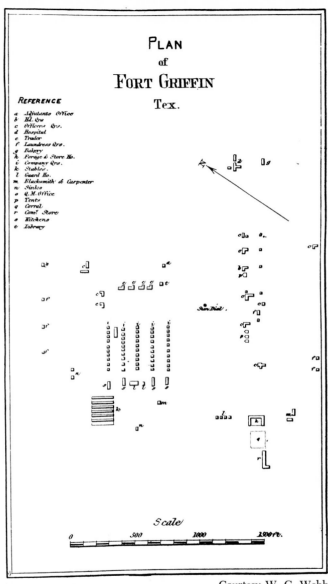

Plan of Fort Griffin

Temporarily the new post was called "Camp Wilson," honoring the memory of the late Lieutenant Wilson, son of a United States senator from Massachusetts. A short time later, however, its name was changed to Fort Griffin, after General Charles Griffin, commander of the Military Department of Texas, 1866–67.[12]

Within a few days the top of "Government Hill" changed. The mesquite brush and prickly pears were cleared away, the trees were uprooted or trimmed, lots were surveyed for the proposed buildings, a flagpole was raised in the center of the new parade ground, a two-room loghouse was hauled up from the now-deserted Maxwell's ranch and used for the commandant's residence, and all about, in orderly fashion, were army tents for the officers and men.

But this work was only preliminary. The depot quartermaster at San Antonio, J. D. C. Lee, presently sent forward heavily laden ox-drawn wagon trains, piled high with materials for the new fort—steam sawmills, window sashes, door frames, and tools. With these supplies came twenty-two carpenters, a building superintendent, masons, and "sawyers"—all under the supervision of Lieutenant H. B. Mellen, acting quartermaster.

Before winter had set in, a line of officers' quarters—a room and kitchen each—made of logs, and forty-two small one-room log huts for the enlisted men—each fourteen and

of Contreras, Churubusco, and Molino del Rey. Later, he again was on the frontier, in Kansas and Indian Territory, and was with Johnson's Utah expedition, 1858–60. He also served with the Thirty-seventh New York Volunteers and other federal organizations operating in the East during the Civil War.

[12] "Medical History of the Post, Fort Griffin, Texas, 1867–81" (MS, A. G. O., War Records Division, National Archives, Washington), 1.

one-half feet long, eight feet wide, and five feet, ten inches high (to the eaves)—were built. In each of these small huts six men were quartered, with no ventilation except from a small window at one end and a door at the other.[13]

In the next year the work on the new post was continued. Alex J. Perry, brevet brigadier general and quartermaster of the army, reported great building progress. Axmen had cut 1,025 oak, elm, and cottonwood logs, from which a portable mill had sawed 83,264 feet of lumber. From this "rawhide" lumber there were built "1 log storehouse, 100 by 18 feet; 2 frame storehouses, 70 by 18 feet; 1 log hospital, 40 by 18 feet; a wing of the hospital, 28 by 16 feet; 1 log quarters for the commanding officer, 38 by 15 feet; 1 frame kitchen, 12 by 20 feet; 2 frame quarters for officers, 32 by 16 feet; 2 frame kitchens, 16 by 20 feet; frame quarters for the post surgeon, 12 by 28 feet; 1 frame kitchen, 12 by 20 feet; 2 frame buildings for first sergeants, 12 by 15 feet; 18 frame company quarters, 8½ by 13 feet; 1 frame stable, 10 by 180 feet."[14] Most of these buildings were lathed and plastered. Yet the entire cost, including the wages of the extra-duty men, was but $22,000, hardly more than that of a present-day six-room house.

The green lumber in these buildings, which were completed by the winter of 1867–68, shrank and warped badly, so much, indeed, that soon extensive repairs had to be made, and the cold winds and rain of midwinter and the sandstorms of spring made life uncomfortable for their occu-

[13] *Ibid.*, 2, 12. Assistant Surgeon Henry McElderry reported that this lack of ventilation was a contributing cause of dysentery, diarrhea, and continued fever.

[14] 40 Cong., 3 sess., *House Ex. Doc. 1*, I, 706, 864.

pants. The cavalry horses suffered most, and some of them died of pneumonia,[15] for stables had not yet been built.

It was difficult to maintain high morale among the enlisted men when their superiors made no effort to improve their crowded housing condition in the earlier-built picket huts, especially when they had to help civilian employees construct better quarters for the commissioned officers.[16] On December 14, 1869, Assistant Surgeon Henry McElderry reported that a new line of officers' quarters had been completed, running northeast and southwest and facing the northwest. The first group of houses on this line consisted of one-story buildings, each containing three rooms and a kitchen in the rear, with a wide fireplace; and two other houses contained four rooms each, a wide hallway, a fireplace, a kitchen, and an underground cellar. Nor was the commandant slighted: he was furnished a two-story structure, with a ground floor of four rooms separated by a hallway, a portico in front and rear, and an underground cellar.

Although the original building plan was to substitute substantial stone buildings for the picket, log, and frame structures, this was never done. Only a few structures—the commissary building, the bakery, the hospital, the powder magazine, and the commanding officer's quarters—were finally built wholly or in part of stone. Other quarters for the assistant surgeon, hospital attendants, laundresses, and

[15] Grant, "The Early History of Shackelford County," as cited, 52; 40 Cong., 3 sess., *House Ex. Doc. 1*, I, 864.

[16] As late as March 3, 1871, the *San Antonio Daily Express* complained that the soldiers were taken away from frontier duty "to erect comfortable quarters for the officers."

noncommissioned officers and their families were built before the post was abandoned.[17]

The three older posts of Belknap, Phantom Hill,[18] and Chadbourne were again brought into use as subposts, the first two of which were garrisoned by small Fort Griffin army units. (Since the buildings at Phantom Hill had been burned after its evacuation in 1854, the men now stationed there were to live in tents.)[19] A Fort Griffin guard was also maintained at Mountain Pass, about forty miles southwest of Phantom Hill. The subpost garrisons were to supply escorts for the stagecoaches carrying mail and passengers from one border post to another, for border patrols, and for government wagon trains and surveying parties operating within the Indian country. In fact, that part of the defense line from Fort Richardson to the Big Bend country, on which Fort Griffin was the most strategic point, was designed to answer the distress call of the Clear Fork and Brazos settlers. Unfortunately, however, mobile cavalry units, most serviceable for Indian warfare, could not be sent in sufficient strength to guard the settlements effectively. And since the troopers available could not screen the frontier, Indian and white raiders could slip past the widely separated posts to rain telling blows on the interior settlements.

[17] "Medical History of the Post, Fort Griffin, Texas, 1867–81," as cited, 16.

[18] Phantom Hill was officially known as "Post on the Clear Fork of the Brazos." For official name see Colonel W. G. Freeman's "Inspection Report, 1853" (MS, Old Files, War Records Division, A. G. O., National Archives, Washington).

[19] "Special Orders, No. 24, 1871–May 5, 1878, Fort Griffin" (MS, Old Files, War Records Division, A. G. O., National Archives, Washington), I, 19.

At Fort Griffin, army life at best was routine and generally unexciting. Bugle calls regulated the day's activities. Reveille was at daybreak; Stables, immediately after; Sick Call, 6:45 A.M.; Breakfast, 7:00; Drill, 7:30; Recall from Drill, 8:30; Fatigue, 8:30; Guardmounting, 9:30; Water Call, 11:15; Orderly Call, 11:45; Recall from Fatigue, 12:00 NOON; and "Dinner," 12:15 P. M. An Afternoon started with Fatigue, 1:00; and then Recall from Fatigue, 4:00; Stables, 4:30; Retreat, SUNDOWN; Fatigue, 8:15; Sunday inspection, at 9:00 A. M.; and Guardmounting, immediately after.[20]

The enlisted men could expect little variation in the breakfast, "dinner," and "supper" bills of fare. At breakfast, they were offered beef, bread, and coffee, the entree occasionally changing to fish balls or mackerel. But generally it was beef, not only for breakfast, but dinner also, although soup (pea, bean, or rice), plum pudding, and vegetables in season were added. Of course, too, they had better fare on the Fourth of July, Thanksgiving, and Christmas. For supper, there was almost uniformly "bread and coffee," sometimes with apples or molasses added.[21]

The officers had better fare. A "List of extra groceries furnished by A. C. S." included breakfast bacon, sugar-

[20] "Medical History of the Post, Fort Griffin, Texas, 1867–81," as cited, 141.

[21] *Ibid.*, 42ff., gives bills of fare for enlisted men. Each company chose its own cook, and its food was good or bad depending on this cook's culinary proficiency. When the troops were on escort or patrol duty, they were generally furnished a flour ration and had to cook their own bread, often adding to their flour mix a liberal amount of baking powder. The dough was cooked in Dutch ovens. As they were novices at bread making, the result was bad. Assistant Surgeon D. G. Caldwell believed that oven-baked bread contributed to diarrhea and other stomach disorders.

cured ham, fish, oysters, vegetables, fruits, jam, jelly, and spices.

If the enlisted man voiced resentment because of his fare, he might be assigned extra duty or sent to the smelly guardhouse. Extra duty often included cleaning the stables and latrines. The latrine assignment was loathsome, although the officers' and hospital "sinks" were reasonably sanitary. These sinks were furnished with movable boxes, lined inside and out with zinc, and each seat was equipped with an upper and lower box, one smaller and shallower than the other and fitting into it. The upper was for offal, the fluid part passing through small holes into the lower box, and through it into the earth. Each morning the contents of the upper boxes must be emptied into barrels and carted away a mile leeward of the post. And once a week the earth about each sink became so saturated with urine that it also had to be dug up and removed and new earth mixed with lime put in its place. The enlisted men's latrines were a short distance back of their huts and were insufferably unsanitary, but no change in them was made for the first two years. Obviously, a guardhouse assignment was to be preferred to latrine duty.[22]

Aside from the regimental band's daily program of music, the enlisted man found little entertainment on "Government Hill," except an occasional visit to the small village below the post or a tramp away from the post. On rainy or cold days, checkers, cards, or other games of chance, or

[22] *Ibid.*, 241. During the 1870's the Assistant Surgeon listed an average of twenty-four guardhouse inmates charged with such offenses as "manslaughter, theft, desertion, and drunkenness." The Assistant Surgeon wrote that as many as fifty-six prisoners were confined to the "badly policed, overcrowded and badly ventilated guardhouse on November 26, 1871."

competitive sports, were indulged in. Occasionally, a soldier visited the post library to while away his time with a book from the fifty-six titles available. Perhaps, too, if he were ill and in the hospital, an indulgent medical officer would permit him to read one or more works from his well-stocked library, often with such titles as Robert Bertholow's *Manual of Instruction for Enlisting and Discharging Soldiers,* John C. Dalton's *Treatise on Human Physiology,* or Samuel D. Gross's *System of Surgery.* [23]

Because of the monotony and the necessity of meeting irksome military requirements, the soldier often sought surcease in commissary whiskey, by means of which his ebullient spirit found release either in merriment or in garrulity and brawls; if the latter, he usually awoke from his "jag" in the guardhouse. During a one-year period Assistant Surgeon Carlos Carvallo treated 150 such patients in the hospital for contusions.[24]

The officers at Fort Griffin had better opportunities to relieve military tedium. At formal post soirees and dances, by horseback riding, at ranch-home dinners and military receptions, they and their wives could find enjoyment. They were generally prompt in meeting their own social obligations. And, of course, the officers had variety in patrol duty or in the pursuit of marauding Indians.

For the Clear Fork frontiersman, Fort Griffin meant government protection. Indeed, the post had a dominating influence over the entire region, so much so that we may refer to it as the Fort Griffin country. Daily its cavalry and infantry were away from "Government Hill" in large and

[23] *Ibid.,* 17ff.
[24] *Ibid.,* 69ff. This was a familiar kind of ailment after the arrival of the Twenty-fourth Regiment of Negroes.

small units, hauling wood and lumber from Mill Creek, escorting mail and passenger stages, and following predatory Indians. And, in turn, near-by settlers came to the fort with eggs, milk, butter, and fresh beef for sale, or to watch the soldiers at drill and inspection. Thus, Fort Griffin became the nerve center of community life until the near-by settlements could be stabilized.

The Tonkawa Indian village near Fort Griffin was a friendly adjunct, for its warriors served as guides of military organizations sent in pursuit of hostile Indians. Tonkawa women also found limited employment about the post and shortly in the wild town below "Government Hill," but their smelly, filthy attire sometimes made them unwelcome in the settlers' homes.

Soon the ranchers scattered along the Clear Fork and its tributaries moved into the neighborhood of the fort for protection and schooling for their children,[25] for a post school was to be available; and within a few months there "was a string of houses" for a mile or more about the post. Government contracts were given the new arrivals for beef, hay, and wood. Hay could be cut and mowed on the lush prairie near at hand, and dense timber was within easy reach. "Uncle Joe" Matthews and other cattlemen supplied the post with beef at $2.75 per one hundred pounds net.

For the first time in many anxious months the settlers could buy at the sutler's store much-needed supplies—canned tomatoes, fruits, oysters, milk (Borden's Eagle Brand), dried fruits, and sperm candles. Thus, not only did Fort Griffin become a market for all the farm and ranch

[25] *Ibid.*, McElderry's entry on December 14, 1869. An enlisted man, serving as foragemaster, kept a school in the post forage house, but after a few months he deserted and fled with government funds and property.

products the settlers had to sell, but its sutler's store also supplied their most urgent wants.[26]

Even more important, however, was the measure of security gained by the settlers from Indian raids, notwithstanding the fact that the warriors visited the vicinity of the fort. Once raiding Comanches killed the son of a prominent settler, a "Mr. Browning," and the other settlers quickly formed a party to go in pursuit. Not far from the fort they came upon a lone Comanche sitting by a fire, roasting a skunk for his dinner. The vengeful white men ordered him to march away from the fire, and as he did so, without turning his head, he was shot in the back, Browning being given the first shot.[27]

Lieutenant Colonel Sturgis sent out strong patrols as soon as he arrived on the Clear Fork. In October, he dispatched Sergeant W. A. T. Ahrberg with forty-five enlisted men and twenty-two Tonk scouts on a patrol through Shackelford, Stephens, and Palo Pinto counties, and he was back at Fort Griffin within a few days, reporting "Indians killed, 3; prisoners taken, 1 woman; property captured, 19 horses, 1 mule, and 2 revolvers"—plus the discovery of the remains of five white men who had been killed by the Indians.[28]

Ordinarily, on short trips from the post, such patrols were unsuccessful. On January 3, 1868, First Lieutenant G. Schreyer, with twenty enlisted men of the Sixth Cavalry, scouted through Shackelford County for a distance of fifty miles, but returned to the post within two days reporting that he had "found no Indian trail."[29]

[26] Matthews, *Interwoven*, 51–52.
[27] *Ibid.*, 41.
[28] 40 Cong., 3 sess., *House Ex. Doc. 1*, I, 712.
[29] *Ibid.*, 713.

Captain Adna R. Chaffee[30] had been at Fort Griffin only a few days when he was ordered to pursue some bold Quahada Comanche raiders, led by a Mexican and a mulatto renegade, who had lain in wait for a Mill Creek wagon train with a weak escort, and when one finally came along, moving toward Fort Griffin, had made their coup with complete success, driving away all the mules of the train.

Sturgis received the report of the affair at 7:30 A.M. on March 5, 1868, and promptly ordered Chaffee to take sixty-two enlisted men of the Sixth Cavalry and seven Tonk scouts and go in pursuit. The pursuers followed the fresh Indian trail at a fast pace, traveling out to Ledbetter's salt works where they picked up the trail, and then westerly and northwesterly to Dead Man's Creek, crossing the Clear Fork below Phantom Hill, and on through Jones and Haskell counties.

When the Comanches observed that they were being followed, they divided into two parties, one consisting of the warriors and the other of young braves in charge of the stolen animals. Chaffee wanted to punish those warriors who would dare stop a government wagon train directly under the muzzles of the fort's guns and steal its mules, so he followed at a gallop the trail of the fleeing warriors. At daylight on the third day of the pursuit, the Tonks found the warriors encamped in the Wichita River

[30] Chaffee was a veteran of the Civil War. On July 22, 1861, he enlisted in the Sixth Cavalry, with which he was connected for twenty-five years. On October 12, 1867, he was commissioned a captain in this regiment and was singularly successful in operations against hostile Indians. During the Spanish-American War, he was cited for bravery in the battle of Santiago, and was a member of the China Relief Expedition which entered Pekin in 1900.

breaks, seeking protection from a cold norther, little suspecting that their pursuers were so close on their heels.

Quickly Chaffee made ready his attack. He sent his
Tonk scouts around the camp to cut off retreat from the
north, and then charged with his cavalry, each cavalryman
armed only with his pistol. The Comanches were thrown
into utter confusion by this encirclement and by the shrill
war whoops of the Tonks, the thunder of horses' hoofs, and
pistol fire. They fought stubbornly to break through the
cordon of charging troopers about them, and finally did so,
but with the loss of seven killed and several wounded.[31]

When Chaffee returned to the post a short time later,
he promptly reported to Lieutenant Colonel Sturgis. Sturgis was greatly pleased. He had been criticized for using
his enlisted men primarily for post building. He could now
report a successful action against Indian raiders. So with
much satisfaction on March 10, he issued his General Order No. 19:

The Commanding Officer takes pleasure in openly announcing
to the troops of this command, the complete success of the detachment that left this post on the 6th instant, under command
of A. R. Chaffee, Sixth United States Cavalry. This short and
decisive campaign has resulted in the killing of five Indians
and one Mexican and one mulatto (both of whom were leaders),
the capture of five horses, together with a large number of
shields, bows and arrows, etc., and the total breaking up of an
Indian camp which had for a long time been a scourge to the
people of the frontier.

[31] "Annual Report, Department of Texas for 1868" (MS, War Rec-
ords Division, A. G. O., National Archives, Washington); "Return of the
Sixth Regiment of the United States Cavalry," March, 1868 (MS, War
Records Division, A. G. O., National Archives, Washington).

The casualties on our side were three wounded, viz.: Privates John F. Butler and Charles Hoffman of Troop I, and Private James Regan of Troop E. With the exception of the wounds of these men, the result is extremely gratifying, as was also the soldierly manner in which the troops bore their deprivations throughout the pursuit, suffering from the cold storm that raged throughout the entire march, without a murmur of discontent.

In all campaigns where important results are achieved and especially against Indians, where the nature of the country is not well known, troops must expect to undergo hardships and deprivations, which cannot be foreseen or obviated; yet it is only the true soldiers who accept these inconveniences as necessary and unavoidable and who like men, maintain their spirit in spite of these.[32]

More than once, stampeding buffalo interfered with the work of pursuing troopers. On July 8, 1870, a force of thirty-seven enlisted men and ten Tonk scouts left Fort Griffin in pursuit of Indian marauders. They overtook them far west of Phantom Hill and engaged them in a sharp battle, in which one Indian was killed and a herd of cattle was captured and turned back toward the range from which it was driven. But in the fight, the Indians escaped and were again pursued by the troopers. The trail was finally lost, however, when a herd of buffalo stampeded and crossed between the pursued and the pursuers. The tired troopers returned to Fort Griffin on July 22, 1870, to report only partial success for their mission.[33]

[32] "General Orders, Fort Griffin, Texas" (MS, War Records Division, A.G.O., National Archives, Washington); 40 Cong., 3 sess., *House Ex. Doc. 1,* I, 213.

[33] "Expeditions and Scouts," Department of Texas, 1870 (MS, War Records Division, A.G.O., National Archives, Washington).

V Chasing Kiowas and Quahadas

D URING THE WINTER of 1870–71, Kiowa and Comanche war parties repeatedly ravaged the Texas border,
so that Governor Edmond J. Davis complained that "the
atrocities recently committed by the Indians" were even
beyond "all previous experience of their murderous doings."

The Santa Fé *Daily New Mexican* of October 21, 1870,
had carried a *San Antonio Express* news item devoted to
these stepped-up Indian raids, stating that three days
earlier "Kicking Bird, Little Heart, Satank, Timbered
Mountain and Lone Wolf, with all their Kiowa braves and
families and lodges and ponies," had arrived at Fort Sill.
They had brought with them a Mrs. Koozer and her five
children, whom they had captured at Henrietta, Texas, on
the Little Wichita, in the preceding July, and demanded
that General B. H. Grierson pay them five hundred dollars
apiece for their captives, but, instead, the General forced
them to surrender the mother and children without ransom.

"Before leaving," continued this news item, "the Indians placed White Horse, a candidate for chieftainship,
in front of the council [the assembled Indians and Grier-

son and his fellow officers] and said . . . : 'This is the great brave who lately stole the seventy mules right from under your noses, and scalped the three men near this post, and shot into the cattle herd, and had your soldiers wild and running all over the country to catch them. We want to make him a chief for these things. He is the man that captured the women and children and killed Mr. Koozer in Texas . . . and was the greatest brave in June and July and has killed many Texans, and burned many houses, and laid waste much country—make him a Kiowa Chief." Of course, Grierson did not comply.

On January 24 of the next year, four Negroes hauling supplies from Weatherford to Fort Griffin were on the Butterfield Trail, two miles south of Flat Top Mountain, in Young County, when a band of Kiowas led by Maman-ti and Quitan charged them from a near-by wooded hiding place. One of the freighters, Brit Johnson, who had secured the release of captives taken during the Elm Creek raid of 1864, immediately took command of the defenders. He and his comrades killed their horses and used them as barricades, but all to no purpose. Within a few minutes the Negroes were killed and scalped and the Indians with their bloody tokens of victory were riding back toward Red River, amusing themselves by tossing the kinky-haired scalps at one another. Finally they tired of this sport and threw the scalps away, as the hair on them was too short to be of great value.[1]

A few hours later Second Lieutenant W. A. Borthwick led a small detachment of the Sixth Cavalry out of Fort Richardson to bury the dead Negroes and to pursue and

[1] *Army and Navy Journal* (May 13, 1871); Nye, *Carbine and Lance,* 158.

punish the red invaders. He accomplished his first mission, but when he overtook the Kiowas, leisurely riding toward Red River, and engaged them in a fight, he was wounded and he and his men were driven back to the fort.

Such truculence, savagery, and mounting Indian raids brought General William Tecumseh Sherman to the Texas frontier to see for himself whether or not the Texas settlers' constant clamor for protection was justified.

Sherman, his staff, a military escort, and R. B. Marcy, now the inspector general of the army, arrived at Fort Griffin on May 15, 1871, having traveled via Forts Mc-Kavett, Concho, Chadbourne, and Phantom Hill. Although this was Sherman's first visit to the Clear Fork country, Marcy could well remember his earlier experiences in exploring this region and helping to locate the Clear Fork Comanche reservation.[2]

Neither Sherman nor Marcy was impressed with Fort Griffin as a permanent border post. Sherman thought that Griffin and Richardson were "not well placed unless the settlers were willing to retreat before the Indians." Old Camp Cooper and "a point near the head of Little Wichita would make a shorter line"[3] in connection with Fort Sill. Inspector General Marcy was much concerned to find that Fort Griffin was not on government land. "Thus far," he said, "no considerable expenditures in buildings had been incurred here, and with the exception of three small framed

[2] Inspector General Marcy's "Journal," in W. T. Sherman's Official Papers (MS, Library of Congress, Washington), I, February 11, 1866–February 8, 1878. See in particular, entry of May 15, 1871.

[3] Sherman to Adjutant General E. D. Townsend, May 24, 1871 (MS in Division of War Records, A. G. O., National Archives, Washington).

houses for officers, the buildings are mere temporary log or board cabins."[4]

Next day Sherman and Marcy with a cavalry escort resumed their journey to Fort Richardson, traveling by way of the old Fort Belknap road. Beyond the Clear Fork they became lost, and W. D. Howsley, a local citizen, rode with them about ten miles back to the right road, for which service Sherman paid him ten dollars. At Belknap and beyond they found increasing signs of Indian devastations—lone chimneys, where houses had been burned, and hastily abandoned fields. At one point Marcy made the observation, "This rich and beautiful section does not contain today so many white people as it did when I visited it eighteen years ago, and if the Indian marauders are not punished, the whole country seems to be in a fair way of becoming totally depopulated."[5]

Hardly had the two men reached Fort Richardson when they learned of a near-by Kiowa raid on Henry Warren's wagon train bringing shelled corn from Fort Richardson to Fort Griffin. Indeed, the Sherman-Marcy party had but a few hours before traveled over this same road past the massacre site. On May 19, Sherman wrote to Major W. H. Wood at Fort Griffin, giving him a succinct account of the affair. "A pretty strong party of Indians have attacked and captured a train of twelve (12) wagons this side of Salt Creek—killed seven men, and five (5) have escaped to this post—one (1) wounded." He ordered Wood to take 150 cavalry men and join Colonel Ranald S. Mackenzie in

---

[4] Marcy's "Journal," as cited. Marcy was in error about the number of frame houses. See 40 Cong., 3 sess., *House Ex. Doc. 1*, I, 706, 864.

[5] Marcy's "Journal," as cited. See, in particular, entry of May 17, 1871.

pursuit of the marauders. Wood was to strike for the head of Little Wichita, to scout around its tributaries, and to attack any party of Indians he found. Mackenzie's command had already moved out from Fort Richardson.[6]

Mackenzie, commanding Fort Richardson, had previously received orders to go in pursuit of the Indians with all his available cavalry. If the Indians had crossed Red River, he was to enter the Comanche-Kiowa reservation, "and if the trail be fresh," his orders ran, "and you should overtake the party anywhere within thirty or forty miles of Red River, you will not hesitate to attack the party, secure the property stolen, and any other property or stock in their possession, and bring them to me at Fort Sill."[7]

The news of the Kiowa raid was soon known in the Fort Griffin country. Susan Newcomb wrote a fairly accurate diary account of what had happened. There were ten wagons, twelve men, and forty mules in Warren's wagon train, she said. Seven of the men were killed and the others made their escape. The raiders took the wagon sheets, cut open the corn sacks and poured their contents on the ground, and mutilated the teamsters whom they had killed. The feet of one of them were chained together and the body burned, an ax was stuck up to the handle in another's skull,[8] and all were horribly mutilated.

Sherman was now convinced that the many reports he had received earlier about Texas border Indian atrocities were true. But he stoutly maintained that the military had not been remiss in its duty. He charged that the Depart-

[6] Sherman to Wood, May 19, 1871 (MS, Sherman's Official Papers, Library of Congress).

[7] Sherman to Mackenzie, May 19, 1871 (MS, Sherman's Official Papers, Library of Congress).

[8] Susan Newcomb's diary, June 15, 1871.

ment of the Interior had permitted Indian agents to give food, clothing, and shelter to these very Indians while their hands were yet red with blood, and had winked at a wholesale trade in guns and ammunition which Kansas and New Mexico traders were carrying on with the wild Indians. In this connection he wrote to General John Pope, commanding the Department of Missouri: "If from New Mexico you could catch one of those [*Comanchero*] trading caravans that come out by Red River to trade in arms it would be a good thing."[9] There is little doubt that many of the raiders' improved rifles had been procured from *Comancheros.*

Almost immediately after Sherman and his party arrived at Fort Sill they witnessed the sensational arrest of the Texas raid leaders. Sherman had inquired of Agent Lawrie Tatum if any Indians were away from the reservation at that time. Tatum replied that he knew of none, but that he would not be surprised if some of his charges were a hundred miles off, killing citizens and stealing horses and mules, that the Comanches and Kiowas were beyond his control, and that "they come and go as they please."[10]

Three days later, on Saturday morning, May 27, Satanta came to the agency and confessed boastingly to Tatum that he had killed the seven teamsters and had destroyed Warren's train and brought back forty-two mules. He wanted his rations quickly so that he might go out to his village, which was moving up toward the Antelope Hills. Tatum and Interpreter Horace P. Jones persuaded

[9] Sherman to Pope, May 24, 1871 (MS, Sherman's Official Papers, Library of Congress).
[10] Sherman to Sheridan, May 29, 1871 (MS, Sherman's Official Papers, Library of Congress).

him to accompany them to General Grierson's quarters, where a great white chief from Washington was visiting.

Sherman later related to General Phil Sheridan, commanding the Military Division of the Missouri, what happened next. Tatum told him, he wrote, "that he wanted him [Satanta] arrested. I gave the necessary orders and as he [Satanta] observed officers and orderlies moving about, he started for his horse, which was close by, and General Grierson's orderly, the only man then near who was armed, pointed his pistol, and bade him be seated. From that moment he was a prisoner.

"We aimed to get three others [chiefs] who had been with him in Texas," Sherman stated. "We secured two others, Satank and Big Tree, but the fourth, Black Eagle, seeing the movements of the garrison, fled. The camps of those who had come in also stampeded, but we held about a dozen, among them Lone Wolf, Kicking Bird, Stumbling Bear, etc., till I explained to them that the three who were held would be sent back to Texas for trial and hanging. They begged hard to be shot on the spot, but that is too good a fate for them, and I have ordered General Grierson, if Mackenzie comes in here as I expect him, to deliver them to him to be carried back to Fort Richardson, to be tried by the civil authorities there. . . . Old Satank ought to have been shot long ago, and Big Tree is a young warrior, the successor to Faint Heart who died last winter."[11]

Mrs. Newcomb was pleased by Sherman's prompt action. She wrote that he with seventy men had passed along the road where the massacre occurred just ahead of Warren's wagons, and that after he heard the news of the massacre, he sent all the men he could get (soldiers and

[11] *Ibid.*

citizens) "after the red imps of the earth." She added that Warren had accompanied Sherman to Fort Sill to recover his mules, for Sherman had told him that he could "get his pay." "This was more than any other man ever said to a citizen of the frontier," Susan stated. "I say hurray! for General Sherman. . . . I hope he will make much mischief among the Indians."[12]

Meanwhile, Wood's cavalry had joined Mackenzie in his hunt for the Kiowa raiders' trail, but the Kiowas had made their escape to the reservation, to which presently the dispirited troopers came. Here Mackenzie learned for the first time that the ringleaders in the foray had been arrested and were to be sent back to Jacksboro in his custody for trial.

Just as Mackenzie's wagon train started southward, Satank attempted to escape and was shot by one of the mounted guards, but Mackenzie delivered Satanta and Big Tree to Sheriff Michael McMillan of Jack County. They were tried at Jacksboro before Judge Charles Soward, convicted, and sentenced to death. However, the importunities of Enoch Hoag, superintendent of Indian affairs in Kansas, and later Judge Soward and Agent Tatum, caused Governor Davis to commute their sentences to life imprisonment. A short time later they were sent to the Huntsville penitentiary under a heavy guard.[13]

[12] Susan Newcomb's diary, following entry of May 15, 1871.

[13] For a complete coverage of the arrest of the Kiowa chiefs, the death of Satank, the Jacksboro trial, and the commutation of Santana and Big Tree's sentences, see Marcy's "Journal" as cited, the entry of May 27; Sherman to Sheridan, May 29, 1871; Lawrie Tatum, *Our Red Brothers* (Philadelphia, 1899), Chapter IV; James Mooney, "Calendar History of the Kiowa Indians," *Seventeenth Annual Report of the Bureau of American Ethnology, 1895–96* (Washington, 1898), Part I, 188ff.; Carl Coke

Agent Lawrie Tatum had little patience with the Department of the Interior's "peace policy," as expressed in terms of feeding and clothing the wild Indians without holding them to a strict accountability for all their acts of outlawry. He believed that the raiding Comanches and Kiowas should be punished, and he worked in close cooperation with General B. H. Grierson of Fort Sill to that end. But there were yet nomadic incorrigibles ranging the Staked Plains. These had to be driven from their canyon hideouts and out-of-the-way places and forced to submit to reservation control, for they were the worst of the border offenders. The Quahadas, led by Quanah Parker,[14] and particularly the bands of such truculent subchiefs as Mowway (the "Handshaker") and Para-a-coom ("He Bear"), formed the hard core of these irreconcilables, which included outlaws Yamparika and Kotsoteka Comanches and remnants of other bands.

The Quahada chiefs had repeatedly told Tatum that they would not accept reservation control until the "blue coats" (soldiers) invaded their country and whipped them. Only then would they agree to "walk on the white man's road." They scorned the government's annuities, for they could acquire all the white man's goods they needed from the *Comancheros,* the unscrupulous hard-bargaining New

Rister, "The Significance of the Jacksboro Indian Affair of 1871," *The Southwestern Historical Quarterly,* Vol. XXIX (January, 1926), 181–200; "Minutes of the 43rd Judicial District of Texas" in Rister Papers (MS, Texas Technological College Library), Vol. A., 214ff.

[14] Quanah Parker was the son of Peta Nacona, a Nokoni chief, and the Texas captive, Cynthia Ann Parker. Cynthia Ann had been captured by the Indians when in May, 1836, they had attacked "Parker's Fort," near present Groesbeck in Limestone County, Texas. See James T. DeShields, *Cynthia Ann Parker: The Story of Her Capture* (St. Louis, 1886).

Mexicans who periodically met them at such remote retreats as Las Tecóvas or Sanbord Springs, near present Amarillo; Valle de las Lágrimas, or Quitaque; Laguna Sabinas, about fifteen miles northwest of present Lamesa; and Cañon del Rescate, or the Yellow Houses, near present Lubbock. As early as October 25, 1849, James S. Calhoun, superintendent of Indian affairs in New Mexico, had mentioned the infamous New Mexican trade with the Indians. The *Comancheros* not only kept the Indians well supplied with guns and ammunition, but they bought from them women and children captives to resell to anxious parents and relatives. Calhoun stated that the *Comancheros* engaged openly in this illicit trade and went where they pleased "without being subject to the slightest risk."[15] (Indeed, it was about this captive racket that Agent Tatum wrote to Grierson. "I should be very glad," he said, "if thee and General Mackenzie could get that little captive and induce Mow-way and his band to come into this reservation and behave. Mow-way does not appear likely to bring in that poor little captive child of his own volition."[16]

Not long after the Jacksboro trial of Satanta and Big Tree, Major Woods, commanding Fort Griffin, had orders to co-operate with Mackenzie, who was to lead an imposing force of cavalry against the Staked Plains Indian malcontents. Units of Mackenzie's cavalry left Fort Richardson on September 19, 1871, and marched over the Fort Griffin

[15] *The Official Correspondence of James S. Calhoun,* ed. by Annie Heloise Abel (Washington, 1915), 51ff. For more recent discussions of the *Comancheros* see Carl Coke Rister, *Southern Plainsmen* (Norman, 1938), 95–96; J. Evetts Haley, *Charles Goodnight* (Boston and New York, 1936), Chapter XI.

[16] Quoted in Richardson, *Comanche Barrier,* 346.

road to the Clear Fork, and thence up that stream to Camp Cooper, where he concentrated his little army.

For several days Camp Cooper was a beehive of military activity with the arrival of cavalry and infantry and supply trains. By September 25, eight troops of the Fourth Cavalry, four from Fort Richardson, two from Griffin, and two of the Eleventh Infantry from Concho, together with about twenty Tonkawa scouts, were encamped, ready for the long trek into Quahada country. That night a large Indian war party had created a diversion by driving off 120 cattle and 13 horses from Murphy's ranch, about twenty miles away. Captain Wirt Davis, commanding the camp, refused to go in pursuit, as he had orders to remain at Camp Cooper resting his men and horses until Mackenzie's arrival.[17]

Preliminary to the cavalry's westward advance on September 30, Captain R. G. Carter was ordered to take eight men and five Tonks and proceed up the Clear Fork to select a good camp for the troops and then to find a practicable road for Mackenzie's wagon train. Upon his return, on October 3, Mackenzie's entire command of about six hundred men left its "bivouac on the beautiful bend of the Clear Fork," the troopers singing "Come home, John, don't stay long; Come home soon to your own Chick-a-biddy!" The infantry, troops of cavalry, Tonk scouts—six hundred officers and men—and nearly one hundred heavily laden pack mules must have presented a colorful sight as they moved out in a long line. Major E. M. Lawton's wagon train was to follow later.

[17] "Tabular Statement of Expeditions and Scouts, 1871" (MS, 4099, A. G. O., War Records, National Archives, Washington); Captain R. G. Carter, *On the Border with Mackenzie* (Washington, 1935), 158ff.

As shown on a contemporary map,[18] the line of advance westward was across California and Paint creeks, both quicksand streams, to the next night's camp at Cottonwood Springs, a few miles northeast of Double Mountain, which was "in plain sight," where the tired men spent a long-remembered night.

Since their camp was within Indian country, the troopers were ordered to avoid making undue noise. Captain Carter was in charge of the guard that night, including herd guards, "sleeping parties," and all camp guards and picket outposts. At midnight he lay down to rest on a buffalo robe near the sergeant of the picket reserve, but before he could fall asleep, he heard the thunderous noise of stampeding buffalo coming directly toward the camp. His first instinct was to order the guard to fire directly into the mass of oncoming animals, but this would violate Mackenzie's order to avoid making loud noise. Instead, leaping to his feet, he shouted to the sergeant to rout out his guard and

[18] A. R. Roessler's "Latest Map of the State of Texas, 1874," in the archives of the Library of Congress, Washington, D. C. The exact route of the "Mackenzie Trail" as traced on this map shows Mackenzie to have left Camp Cooper and crossed the Clear Fork at Fort Griffin; thence across Collins, Trout, and Limpia creeks and the southwest corner of Throckmorton County, crossing the Clear Fork and California Creek into the southeast part of Haskell County. From there, it ran through southern Haskell County, crossing the Double Mountain Fork and the Salt Fork of the Brazos, approximately twenty miles from their confluence. From here the Trail recrossed Salt Fork to Cottonwood Springs; parallel to the Salt Fork of the Brazos, crossing Salt, Duck, and South Fort creeks. And still paralleling the Salt Fork, it cut the northeastern corner of Garza County and into southeastern Crosby County, and mounted the Staked Plains slightly southeast of present-day Crosbyton, and followed the Blanco Canyon up to Catfish Creek northeast of Crosbyton, where Mackenzie established his camp.

order them to dash forward with their blankets, waving them and yelling, to turn the buffalo aside. This plan worked perfectly, and the rolling mass of brown monsters caromed off to the left of the camp at breakneck speed and thundered off into the black gloom of night.

Next morning, after the call of "Boots and Saddles," Mackenzie's column splashed across the shallow water of the Salt Fork of the Brazos and followed a north-of-west course paralleling the south bank of the river, through present Kent County. The next night's camp was on Duck Creek, where Lawton was to establish a supply base.

From here the column traveled over rolling country covered with mesquite, chaparral, and cactus, through prairie-dog towns and immense herds of buffalo. Soon the company was in wild, broken country. In every direction were lonely buttes and broken, eroded hills—all likely sentinel posts for watching Quahada scouts. Farther on, they came upon some abandoned *Comanchero* hideouts, "curiously built caves in the high banks or bluffs, the earth being propped up or kept in place by a framework of poles."

That night Mackenzie sent his Tonk scouts to locate the Quahada village. From here pack mules could be quickly sent out in any direction. The two companies of the Eleventh Infantry were to be left as a guard, and Mackenzie announced that he would strike out that night after the hostile Indians. Major Henry W. Lawton, a Civil War veteran, was to be left behind to control supply operations.

At midnight Mackenzie and his troopers were in the saddle, but after several hours of trials, tribulations, profanity, bruises, and utter confusion of men and horses, they found themselves in an inky-dark, small box canyon. Hopelessly handicapped by a labyrinth of arroyos, breaks, ra-

vines, and towering rock-walled cliffs, the troopers bivouacked until morning without fires and ate cold "snacks."
At daybreak they were on the move again, skirting what
had been insurmountable bluffs, and at last, at about 9:30
A. M., they arrived at the Freshwater Fork of the Brazos.
Tired and hungry, they unsaddled, built fires, and ate
breakfast, not far from present Dickens.

Here the Tonks came to report that they had found a
trail leading up the canyon to the Quahada village. Promptly Mackenzie moved out, but the Indians had decamped.
After he had spent a fruitless day looking for them, he
bivouacked again, where the Freshwater Fork broke from
Blanco Canyon and found its way to the rough country
below the frowning Caprock.[19]

Realizing that Quahada scouts had been watching him
floundering about these badlands, Mackenzie feared the
loss of his horses and that night ordered his men to "cross
side-line" them, by hobbling one hind foot to the opposite
front foot, and to tie these side-line ropes to picket pins
driven in the ground. But these precautions were not
enough. Before morning, while it was yet quite dark,
mounted Quahadas came racing through the camp, shouting, ringing cowbells, and dragging bouncing and jounc-
ing rawhides—all creating a bedlam of noise to scare the
tethered horses. The troopers, rudely aroused from slum-
ber, fired wildly through the darkness at elusive foes only
dimly seen above the sky line, but their shots went wild.

[19] "Tabular Statement of Expeditions and Scouts, 1871," as cited;
General C. C. Augur's *Annual Report from the Department of Texas,
1872*, in 42 Cong., 3 sess., *House Ex. Doc. 1;* Carter, *On the Border with
Mackenzie*, 62ff.; John H. Dorst, "Ranald Slidell Mackenzie," in *Twen-
tieth Annual Reunion Association Graduates U. S. Military Academy,*
1889.

Next morning they were chagrined to find that they had lost more than sixty horses.

Soon the discomfited troopers were again on the move, eager to retaliate. Carter found and attacked a small party of Quahada horsemen farther up Blanco Canyon, but in a headlong charge he rounded a turn in the canyon and rode upon a much stronger force of warriors, moving toward him. Other troops from Mackenzie's command hastened up and saved him, for his rapid retreat and rear-guard action were hardly enough to escape the oncoming Indians. Before Mackenzie could get his larger force into action, however, the main Quahada band, including the women and children, had escaped from the canyon and had fled across the plains. The troopers followed at a gallop, but just as they were about to overtake the fleeing Indians, a norther, with blinding cold wind, snow, and rain, blew up and forced them to give up the chase.[20]

Although Mackenzie had been outmaneuvered by Quanah Parker and his subordinates, there was some compensation in the thought that he had gained valuable experience and knowledge of the region, which he could use later. But his trials were by no means over. The weather was unseasonably cold, with rain and snow chilling both men and horses to the bone.

While moving back down the canyon, Mackenzie's advance guard came upon two Comanche scouts studying intently the troopers' trail made earlier that day. Quickly the warriors dashed into brush near the base of the canyon wall and began a desperate defense against the encom-

[20] "Tabular Statement of Expeditions and Scouts, 1871," as cited; *Fort Worth Star Telegram,* February 27, March 6, 13, 20, 27, and April 3, 1927.

passing troopers. And while Captain P. M. Boehm and his Tonks were trying to flush them out, Mackenzie arrived and joined in the fight, only to receive an arrow in the leg, which caused him to retire to have Dr. Rufus Choate extract it. The Tonks finally killed and scalped the two Comanches.

Although Mackenzie continued to search for his wily foes, he did not find them; and since he had lost many of his horses because of the bitter weather, in early November he returned to his base near Fort Griffin.[21]

February, 1872, found Mackenzie at Fort Concho planning another expedition against the Staked Plains Indians. In March he re-established his camp on the Freshwater Fork of the Brazos, and began his search for the Indians. Nor was he long in again establishing contact with them. He pursued them as far as Alamogordo, New Mexico, where they escaped him by breaking into small bands and fleeing through the sand hills in many directions. Then Mackenzie returned to his camp on the Freshwater Fork, going by way of Palo Duro Canyon, east of present-day Canyon. This return journey added length to what was soon to be known as the Mackenzie Trail.[22]

Only Kiowa raids had lessened during the cold winter of 1871–72, these warriors waiting to see what the federal authorities would do with Satanta and Big Tree; the Comanches even increased their outrages. Satanta said that he "took hold of that part of the white man's road that gave him breech-loading guns; he did not like the ration of corn

[21] "Tabular Statement of Expeditions and Scouts, 1871," as cited; General Augur's *Report,* as cited, II, 54–60.

[22] See Laragerman's *Map of Texas,* 1879. That part of this trail from Fort Griffin, via the Double Mountain Fork, to the Freshwater Fork of the Brazos, was made on his outbound trip in October, 1871.

—it hurt his teeth." Nor were other Kiowas committed to the white man's ways, Wild Horse later saying, "We slowed down on the raids, but our minds were on it." And while they waited, ambitious White Horse wanted to gain new laurels while Satanta and Big Tree, possible rivals, were in prison. He would lead his braves against the Texas frontier and bring back fine horses, mules, and perhaps a captive or two. Perchance his admittance to the Ko-eet-senko clan would be possible.

White Horse's resolution was crystallized when he learned that his brother Kom-pai-te, impatient of the Kiowa waiting policy, had joined a Comanche raiding party and had been killed in a fight with the L. H. Luckett surveying party in the Fort Belknap country. White Horse felt that he was justified now in organizing a revenge raid, and soon led five warriors and a woman into Texas.[23]

In early June of 1872, Henry Griswold Comstock, who lived about a mile below Fort Griffin, started in a wagon for Dallas to purchase certain supplies which were not available at the Flat. Just before nightfall he arrived at the river crossing near the mouth of King's Creek, sixteen miles below Fort Griffin. Here he found Abel John Lee and his family living in a picket house which a cowman had abandoned. As the water in the river was too high that evening, Comstock pitched camp and hobbled out his mules.

Lee sought to make the traveler welcome, but said that he could not ask him to come to the house for supper, since he had been unable to buy any bread at the Flat. "He didn't have the price," Comstock later wrote. Com-

[23] Nye, *Carbine and Lance,* 197f.

stock then "furnished the flour and they had the lard or bacon fat, and Mrs. Lee certainly knew how to make fritters. Man! I can taste them yet."[24]

A short time later, on the warm Sunday afternoon of June 9, Lee sat in a rocking chair reading a newspaper, enjoying the gentle breeze passing through the hallway connecting the two main rooms of his picket house, not anticipating an Indian raid since Fort Griffin, sixteen miles up the Clear Fork, stood as a barrier.[25]

But White Horse's raiders were even then approaching Lee's house, creeping down the river bed. While Lee rocked to and fro, rifle fire burst from a near-by bush thicket and the old man slumped from his chair dead, his body falling across the doorway of the room in which were other members of the family. Quickly the raiders rushed to the house and began their work of death. When they leaped over Lee's body and rushed into the room, Mrs. Lee and her children were gathered, horror-stricken, in one corner. Mrs. Lee started to flee, but fell mortally wounded with an arrow in her back. Then two of the raiders pounced upon her, scalped her, and further mutilated her body.

The Lee children also made a futile attempt to escape through a corn patch, but Frances, aged fourteen, fell, suffering her mother's fate. Millie, nine, stopped to help her dying sister and was captured; Susanna and John, aged seventeen and six, were hunted down in near-by bushes and also captured.

In a matter of minutes the work of death and plunder

[24] B. Comstock to J. R. Webb, August 9, 1952 (MS in W. G. Webb Papers, Albany, Texas).

[25] "Medical History of the Post, Fort Griffin, Texas, 1867–81," as cited, 272.

was over. But before leaving, the raiders shot a few more arrows into Abel Lee's body to ensure his death, rifled the house of everything they could conveniently carry away, mounted their terror-stricken captives on horses, and rode away hurriedly. Before other settlers learned of the attack, the Kiowas had crossed Red River and had returned to their Rainy Mountain village.

Next day, Lieutenant E. C. Gilbreath and a squad of ten troopers and two Tonks came out to investigate the affair. The Clear Fork was full of turbulent water because of a heavy rain the previous night and the soldiers could not cross, but Gilbreath learned the details of the tragedy by shouting across to sorrowful neighbors who were wrapping the dead bodies in quilts and burying them.

According to Captain W. S. Nye, who heard Stumbling Bear, George Hunt, and aged Kiowas tell the tribal word-of-mouth traditions about the raid, the entire village received the returning raiders as conquering heroes and honored them with an all-night dance. White Horse's mother forced the still grieving and tired Susanna to carry water for the celebrants, and, finally, to take part in the scalp-dance. Next day, Susanna and the other Lee captives were given as slaves to various members of the tribe.[26]

On September 29, Mackenzie made a surprise attack on Mow-way's village of 262 lodges on McClellan's Creek, seven miles above its confluence with the North Fork of the Brazos, which his scouts had discovered. He killed 20 warriors, captured 130 women and children and 3,000

---

[26] Tatum, *Our Red Brothers*, 125; Nye, *Carbine and Lance*, 197f.; Rye, *The Quirt and the Spur*, 351–52; Augur's *Report*, as cited. The Lee children were ransomed several months later.

horses, with a loss of but 1 trooper killed and 3 wounded.[27] That night, however, for the second time the Quahadas raided his camp, recovering their horses and taking others belonging to Mackenzie's camp as well. A Texas lad, whom the Indians held as a captive, later stated that when Mackenzie's men attacked Mow-way's camp, they also killed women, young and old, and babies.[28]

After his fight with the Quahadas, Mackenzie returned to Fort Griffin with his prisoners and camped near the post. The Flat turned out to meet the returning heroes and their captives, and the schoolteacher, who presided over fifteen children in a small box structure on the eastern edge of the village, dismissed his small flock to see the captured Indians. J. R. Gilbert, who described the scene in later years, was one of his pupils. Another was little Lottie Durgan, granddaughter of Mrs. Clifton, both of whom Brit Johnson had previously recovered from the Kiowas.

Gilbert said that before the Kiowas would agree to part with Lottie, several old Kiowa women had held her while some young girls tattooed a circle on her forehead, so that they would know her if they should ever see her again. Now, when the captives saw her among the school children, wrote Gilbert, "all the old squaws grabbed her and held her and cried" with happiness, for she yet bore the blue circle on her forehead.[29]

[27] Edward S. Wallace, "General Ranald Slidell Mackenzie—Indian Fighting Cavalryman," *The Southwestern Historical Quarterly,* Vol. LVI (January, 1953), 387–88; Sheridan, *Record of Engagements,* 36.

[28] Clinton L. Smith and Jefferson D. Smith, *The Boy Captives* (Bandera, Texas, 1927), 127–32.

[29] J. R. Gilbert to J. R. Webb, June 14, 1948 (MS in W. G. Webb Papers, Albany, Texas).

Courtesy Muriel H. Wright

Quanah Parker

A short time later Mackenzie transferred the captives to Fort Concho, where they were held in a stockade until they were returned to their Fort Sill reservation. Events shaping up north of Red River soon made this possible.

VI The Great Indian Roundup

M<small>ACKENZIE'S QUAHADA CAMPAIGN</small> of 1872 by no means solved the Indian raiding problem, although the Staked Plains Indian leaders admitted that they had been "whipped." Yet the Fort Griffin country settlers were skeptical; they did not believe that the nomadic warriors would easily give up their thieving habits. For many decades, plunder and theft had supplied many of the Indians' material wants. Tension therefore continued high along both the Clear Fork frontier and within the western Indian Territory Indian villages.

Commissioner Edward P. Smith endorsed the peace policy of the Friends' (Quaker) Indian Committee. President U. S. Grant also accepted it and appointed Henry Alvord, recently a captain of the Tenth Cavalry (Negroes), and Professor Edward Parrish of Philadelphia as special commissioners to escort the nomadic Indian delegates to Washington. Federal officials believed that if these Indians could see the white people's power and wealth, they would favor peace.

When Alvord counseled with the Quahadas and Kotsotekas about adding delegates to his Washington-bound Indian party, he met with a rebuff. Their chiefs stated that although they expected to remain at peace with Washington, they preferred to continue their prairie life. Mow-way disdainfully replied that when the reservation Indians fared better than the wandering prairie bands, then it would be time enough to travel on Father Washington's road.

But finally the special commissioners assembled their delegation and started for Washington. At St. Louis, the Kiowa members were permitted to see and talk to Satanta and Big Tree, who had been brought up from the Texas prison under a military guard commanded by Captain R. G. Carter.

In Washington, the Indians were royally welcomed and given every consideration. They were shown the armed and economic might of the nation, and some of them were impressed with what they saw and heard. Francis A. Walker, commissioner of Indian affairs, promised the visiting Kiowas that if their tribe remained at peace, surrendered all their captives, and gave up their stolen horses and mules, Satanta and Big Tree would be freed. Although only Governor Davis could pardon these prisoners, Walker evidently planned to persuade him to do so. Some of the delegates returned home still believing that their old ways were best, and their Indian Territory brethren were equally stubborn about accepting the white man's ways. Ten Bears counseled peace, but his people spurned his advice. A short time later, he died, unhappy and disowned.[1]

[1] *Annual Report of the Commissioner of Indian Affairs, 1872* (Washington, 1872), 128–48; Henry Alvord's report "Central Superintendency, 1872" (MS in O. I. A., National Archives, Washington).

Since the Indian delegates' favorable report on what they had seen and heard in Washington had not met with general Comanche and Kiowa approval, the "peace policy" advocates sought other means to advance their cause. Leading Quakers renewed their plea for the freeing of Satanta and Big Tree and for restoring the Comanche women and children to their villages. But Tatum was opposed to immediate action. He regarded the government's promise to release Satanta, a daring and treacherous chief, as being "like a dark and rolling cloud on the Western horizon."[2] He urged that, instead of freeing him, other raiding chiefs should be arrested and sent to the penitentiary.

At the Comanche-Kiowa agency, Tatum became increasingly abrupt in dealing with refractory chiefs, much to the displeasure of his superior, Superintendent Enoch Hoag, and the Friends' Indian Committee. He had concluded that these nomads could not be forced to become sedentary farmers; they had followed the hunting and war trails too long to accept readily "the white man's road."

Mackenzie had heard disquieting reports. He had learned that Quahada camps on the Staked Plains were refuges for other disgruntled and untamed Indians, just as old Camp Cooper had been during the late 1850's. These bands were under the bad influence of outlaw *Comanchero* and Anglo-American traders. Indeed, in the McClellan Creek fight, Tatum had reported that "a white man about forty years old, who fought desperately," and twenty Indian warriors were slain.[3]

The Quahadas not only admitted that they had been defeated, but reluctantly accepted their reservation.

[2] Tatum, *Our Red Brothers,* 160.
[3] *Ibid.,* 134.

Henceforth they would send their children to school, and they would even try farming, notwithstanding the fact that they had always depended on nature's bounty. They also asked Tatum to tell Mackenzie that they were now at peace and did not plan other Texas forays.[4] That they were stalling for time was soon evident, for within a few months they joined other Indians to make war on the Texas settlers.

Tatum explained that the Comanches and Kiowas had been reasonably quiet during 1872 and a part of 1873 only because he had employed military force, and that the government yet held more than one hundred of their women and children as prisoners. Also, he said, three Kiowa chiefs had been arrested, one of whom had been killed and the other two, Satanta and Big Tree, were in the Huntsville, Texas, penitentiary; and he had displaced three other chiefs. These stern measures had checked Indian forays.

Reservation Indians also sparred for time. After the Lee captives had been brought to White Horse's village, Tatum demanded their immediate release. The Kiowas held a "big talk" about the matter and agreed to give them up, but they demanded that Tatum at least ransom the girls. "I told them that paying for them was an encouragement to steal more," Tatum said. "They should not have a dollar, and . . . they could have no more rations until the [Lee] boy was [also] brought in."

This statement had in it a new policy; Tatum would neither buy white captives nor issue rations to kidnapers. When he threatened to call for military force, the Kiowas surrendered the Lee captives. "These sisters," Tatum said later, "were the first captives recovered from the Kiowas without paying from $100 to $1,500 for each one."[5] Thomas

[4] *Ibid.*, 137ff.   [5] *Ibid.*, 127.

C. Battey, the Quaker schoolteacher among the Kiowas, wrote of the effectiveness of the new policy in April, 1873, saying that within a little more than a year, Tatum had forced the Comanches and Kiowas to return to him without pay 18 captives and 164 horses and mules.[6]

Superintendent Enoch Hoag thought that Tatum was too severe, and on July 25, 1872, he sent his clerk Cyrus Beede to talk peace with the chiefs and head men of all the Indian Territory tribes. A council was held at Fort Cobb. Agent John D. Miles came from Darlington with leading Cheyennes and Arapahoes, as did the Wichita Agent Johnathan Richards with Caddoes, Wichitas, and Delawares. Tatum and Interpreter Jones drove up from Fort Sill.

These representatives discussed reservation problems at length. Spokesmen of the Five Civilized Tribes urged their nomadic kin to forsake their wild ways and walk on the white man's road, but to no avail. Outside the council Lone Wolf warned that he would not stop raiding the Texas frontier; plundering the settlements was the Kiowas' legitimate occupation. Other Kiowa arrivals brought word that White Horse also spurned peace; he and his warriors would raid when and where they pleased. Of course, these views were soon carried to the council and caused excitement.

Beede had hoped to accomplish much through peaceful persuasion; now, however, he angrily threatened to use armed troops to force the western tribes to accept reser-

---

[6] Carl Coke Rister, *Border Captives* (Norman, 1940), 177; Battey, *Quaker among the Indians,* 138. For the application of Tatum's new policy, see Scofield to Tatum, January 5, 1872 (MS in "Capt., C–K," Federal Archives Division, Oklahoma Historical Building, Oklahoma City) and C. C. Augur to John P. Hatch (MS in "Capt., C–K," Federal Archives Division, Oklahoma Historical Building, Oklahoma City).

vation life. But the Comanches refused to be intimidated, and the conference broke up in confusion.

Thus, at last Tatum had come to an open break with his superiors; poor in health and deeply disappointed, he resigned on March 31, 1873, in favor of a peace-policy Quaker, James M. Haworth.

In line with Haworth's new policy, on June 10, 1873, the Fort Concho commandant sent the Comanche women and children captives to Fort Sill under heavy guard. The military escort was commanded by Captain Robert McClermont. He formally released the prisoners at Fort Sill, "to the great joy of all the tribe." The women captives reported that they had been well fed and treated kindly. The Comanche chiefs and warriors expressed their gratitude. They shook hands with McClermont and some of them gave him a Comanche hug, completely overcome with emotion. They also gave Agent Haworth repeated assurances that they would continue their good behavior.

No doubt, McClermont now felt that friendly Comanche assurances justified him in having deceived angry settlers while he was approaching Jacksboro recently with his prisoners. While on the road he had been warned that the Jacksboro country swarmed with armed and angry men, who were out to oppose the return of the captives. He had sent his captive-laden wagons, together with their armed escort, on a circuitous route around Jacksboro, while he drove his own ambulance into town, pretending to await their arrival. After waiting for more than an hour, he feigned anxiety and drove back over the road to see what had detained them. But while the milling, angry settlers awaited his return, his military guard and wagons were rapidly approaching Red River, beyond successful pursuit. Thus McClermont's strategy had undoubtedly prevented an armed clash.

The release of the Comanche captives encouraged the Kiowas to renew their demand for the freedom of Satanta and Big Tree, and Commissioner Walker urged Governor Davis to accede to their wishes. Satanta had also appealed to Quaker peace-policy advocates to work for his release. He promised that if he were freed, he would see to it that all Indian raiding in Texas would end. Tatum did not believe him. "My candid opinion of him," he wrote, "is that he could not keep the other Indians from raiding if he wished to; and that he would not do it if he could."[7]

Texas settlers were alarmed because of the rising demand to free the two Kiowas and protested to the State Legislature against such a move. The House of Representatives was quick to respond; it voted sixty-two "ayes" to no "nays" to ask Davis not to grant pardons to the two imprisoned chiefs.[8]

Edward P. Smith, successor to Walker as commissioner of Indian affairs, persuaded Governor Davis to bring the prisoners to Fort Sill and to discuss their final disposition with him. The council convened on October 6, 1873. Davis was piqued because Smith had maneuvered him into coming to Fort Sill; therefore, he sought to lay down such hard conditions for Satanta and Big Tree's release that Smith could not meet them.

He demanded that the federal government put a white man in every Indian village to watch and to report on the warriors' behavior. Each Indian must draw his own rations,

[7] Tatum, *Our Red Brothers*, 132–33.
[8] *Journal of the House of Representatives of the 13th Legislature of Texas*, January 14, 1873. Resolutions introduced by Representative Veale.

instead of the chief, as heretofore, every three days. And at that time each must answer to a roll call. Each must also agree to assist in arresting depredating Indians, give up their guns, horses, and mules, and raise cattle, hogs, and corn, like sedentary Indians. For the present, Satanta and Big Tree must be kept in the Fort Sill guardhouse, to be released only when their tribe promised to do these things. Even then, it must be understood that they would be arrested and returned to the Texas penitentiary if their tribe renewed hostilities.

But next day, Smith persuaded Davis to drop all but his last condition, and even it was modified. Davis agreed to free the prisoners immediately, but said that if they should later renew their attacks on the border and oppose the government's reservation policies, they must be returned to the Texas penitentiary. He also asked that the military attempt to arrest at least five of the recent raiders to take the places of Satanta and Big Tree in prison. Smith accepted these conditions, although Haworth and the military authorities were never able to identify, and to arrest, the five guilty raiders. The Comanche chief, Cheavers, and some of his young braves had gone with a detachment of troops to Texas to search for the Comanche raiders, but they soon returned to report no success.[9]

The Kiowas were jubilant to have their chiefs freed. Satanta and Big Tree embraced Governor Davis and gave assurances to Agent Haworth that they would support his reservation policy.

[9] Peggy Joyce Terrell, "Colonel R. S. Mackenzie's Campaigns against the Southern Plains Indians, 1865–1875" (unpublished Master's thesis, Texas Technological College, 1953), 67; James Haworth's *Report* in 43 Cong., 2 sess., *House Ex. Doc. 1*, V, 527.

When General Sherman learned of the Fort Sill agreement, he wrote Davis a stinging letter. "I believe in making a tour of your frontier with a small escort," he said, "I ran the risk of my life and I said to the Military Command what I now say to you, that I will not again voluntarily assume that risk in the interest of your frontier, that I believe Satanta and Big Tree will have their revenge if they have not already had it, and that if they are to have scalps, that yours is the first that should be taken."[10]

Davis replied heatedly. He contended that the Satanta–Big Tree trial at Jacksboro was a judicial error; Texas courts did not have jurisdiction. Why, he asked, were not these Indians tried by a federal military commission while they were Sherman's prisoners at Fort Sill? He believed, he wrote caustically, that nobody should be scalped, "unless it is the man who has forgotten the injunction of his school-book lesson to think twice before speaking once."[11]

But events soon proved that Sherman's criticism was justified. By midsummer of 1874, Comanche and Kiowa depredations had increased alarmingly. During 1873, sixteen persons had been killed, five wounded, and one captured, but in 1874 sixty-five were killed, five wounded, and one captured. This increase in casualties caused Commissioner Walker to renounce peaceful persuasion. He stated that so long as Satanta and Big Tree were in the Texas penitentiary most of the Kiowas had not engaged in Texas

[10] Sherman to Emund J. Davis, February 16, 1874 (MS in Semi-official Letters, 1872–78, Division of Manuscripts, Library of Congress).
[11] Davis to Sherman, February 27, 1874 (MS in Semiofficial Letters, 1872–78, Division of Manuscripts, Library of Congress).

raids; but that now, after their two chiefs had been freed, they had joined other disgruntled Indians in warfare.

General C. C. Augur, commanding the Department of Texas, joined Walker in condemning the new atrocities. "All these outrages," he charged, "were committed by Indians belonging to the Fort Sill reservation, where they are fed by the government and officially regarded as friendly, and their pursuit and punishment within the limits of their reservation prohibited."[12]

Comanche and Kiowa atrocities in western Kansas, eastern Colorado and New Mexico, and particularly in western Texas, brought a storm of settler protests. All complainers urged stern military action.

The Clear Fork settlers had already expressed their anger because of a near-by raid, in July, 1873, when a Fort Griffin cavalry unit had failed to find and punish the marauders. The Indians had attacked a settler's home near Camp Colorado, had killed a Mrs. Williams, and had captured her seven-year-old daughter. A short time later, Captain G. W. Angel's surveying party had found the girl's body, scalped and hanging by the neck to a wild China tree on the Salt Fork of the Brazos, and near by, the child's scalp attached to an Indian shield.[13]

Federal authorities could not condone or defend such an Indian outrage. In a true sense, Indian Bureau officials had too long held out an olive branch to nomadic Indian

[12] C. C. Augur's "Annual Report, 1874" (MS in "Old Files," A. G. O., Division of War Records, National Archives, Washington).

[13] "List of persons killed, wounded, or captured, Department of Texas, during the year ending September 30, 1873" (MS, File No. 5228, 52 A. G. O., Division of War Records, National Archives, Washington). This list accompanies Augur's report.

raiders and had offered them inducement to accept federal supervision. But the warring chiefs had spurned all reasonable peace proposals. Now the military must use the sharp edge of the sword.

Reluctantly, President Grant sanctioned this new policy. Preliminary to its implementation, Satanta was again arrested at the Darlington Cheyenne-Arapaho Agency for violating his parole by supporting the renewal of hostilities and was returned to the Texas penitentiary. There he committed suicide a short time later by leaping from a second-story hospital window.[14] Big Tree avoided arrest by flight to a retreat west of the Wichita Mountains.

Officers at Fort Sill observed the Comanches' and Kiowas' rising spirit of hostility in the latter part of 1873 and the first part of 1874, although Kicking Bird and a few old chiefs still counseled peace. The young chiefs and warriors had not only renewed their thieving forays on the Kansas and Texas frontiers, but they had connived with other tribal elements to stage an all-out war on the whites. The buffalo hunters on their former ranges, destroying their vast bison herds (their commissary), had left them only one or two alternatives: they must either drive both the hunters and the settlers from the country, or they must accept, once and for all time, reservation life.

The young chiefs and warriors chose war to the finish. They staged a grand Sun Dance at Tso'kakan, near the confluence of Elk Creek and the North Fork of Red River,[15] at which were present chiefs and leading warriors of several tribes. The "medicine" pipe was smoked by all—Coman-

[14] *Governor's Message—Coke to Ross, 1871–1891*, 101.
[15] Mooney, "Calendar History of the Kiowas," *Seventeenth Annual Report of the Bureau of American Ethnology, 1895–96*, Part I, 338.

ches, Kiowas, Cheyennes, Arapahoes, and Mescalero Apaches.

At the medicine dance, Esa-tai, a Quahada medicine man, was most influential. He convinced the attending braves of his mysterious powers to raise the dead, to produce vast quantities of cartridges from his stomach, and to so influence the white men that they would not injure the Indians. He told the warriors that the Great Spirit had revealed to him that they must avenge the death of those Indians who were recently killed in Texas. Their first attack, however, should be on the Fort Griffin Tonkawas, and their next on the buffalo hunters at Adobe Walls on the Canadian. His listeners accepted this suggestion, but before it could be executed, Indian spies apprised Colonel Buell of it and the Tonkawas were brought to Fort Griffin for protection.[16]

Then, the Indians planned an attack on the buffalo hunters. Esa-tai assured them that if they would do this, the Great Spirit would shield them from harm. Promptly, the Comanches, Southern Cheyennes, and Kiowas accepted the idea and left for Adobe Walls.

In the early morning hours of June 27, 1874, this combined force of about seven hundred braves sought to overwhelm the thirty-eight hunters behind their earthen protection and to destroy their supply base. Fred Leonard, who aided in the defense of Adobe Walls, wrote to Charley Myers, on July 1, about this perilous position. "We have been attacked by the Indians and corralled since June 27th," he said. "The attack was made early in the morning, and the battle lasted about three hours. Ike Shadler and

[16] *Annual Report of the Commissioner of Indian Affairs, 1874* (Washington, 1874), 220.

Brother, Billy Tyler, and Mr. Olds were killed. The latter shot himself accidentally. . . . The hunters are all sick of hunting, so they say, and are apt to leave without a moment's warning; but I am willing to stay if I can get sufficient men to guard the place. . . . We had to do our fighting from the store. About twenty-five or thirty Indians were killed—we found eleven.[17] . . . If you can get an escort of fifty men, send Anthony's, or all the horse teams you can get."[18]

But reinforcements were not needed. Everywhere about the sodhouse store were wounded and dead Indians, evidence enough that Esa-tai's "medicine" was bad. Reluctantly, the warriors broke off the attack and withdrew. When a detachment of troops inspected the scene on August 19, they found the heads of twelve warriors on the corral pickets, a grim reminder to the ambitious braves that it would be expensive to drive the buffalo hunters from the Staked Plains.

Even earlier General Phil Sheridan, now Sherman's successor as commander of all Trans-Mississippi forces, had been convinced that the die was cast—the hostile Indians must be coerced. He wrote Sherman, now lieutenant general, that the raiders should be punished after they had returned with plunder to their reservations. "It is my opin-

[17] Nelson A. Miles, *Personal Recollections* (Chicago, 1896), 160; Mooney, "Calendar History of the Kiowas," *Seventeenth Annual Report of the Bureau of American Ethnology, 1895-96,* Part I, 203. Agent Haworth reported on September 1, 1874, that "six Comanches and five Cheyennes were killed, one Comanche dying after from wounds. . . . This fight seemed to dispel the influence of the medicine-man." See *Annual Report of the Commissioner of Indian Affairs, 1874,* 220.

[18] Leonard's letter was published in the *Kansas Star Record,* July 15, 1874.

ion these raids only can be stopped," he added, "by a complete control of the reservations. With this control, I would agree inside of eighteen months to close up all Indian troubles forever."[19] Secretary of War W. W. Belknap instructed Sherman to give Sheridan this authority,[20] and a short time later military commanders in Colorado, Kansas, Indian Territory, New Mexico, and Texas had put troops in the field.

In keeping with this policy, by the midsummer of 1874 the agents of the Comanche-Kiowa and Cheyenne-Arapaho reservations had ordered all their Indians to declare themselves either for peace or war; if for the latter, they must stay away from their agency. If they desired reservation protection during the forthcoming military campaign, they must enroll with their agent and receive instructions.[21] But few did so—at Fort Sill, only 173 Kiowas, 108 Katakas (Kiowa-Apaches), and 83 Comanches.

In July, Lieutenant Colonel Davidson supported the agents' policy by announcing that after August 3 all Indians not on their reservations would be declared hostile and liable to attack by his troops. This announcement evidently impressed some of the Comanches, for a short time later Chiefs Big Red Food, Tabernanca, Assanonica, Little Crow, and Black Duck offered to return to the reservation. Only Assanonica, however, was allowed to do so, for the others had taken part in the Adobe Walls fight.

[19] Sheridan to Sherman, August 12, 1873 (MS, Sheridan Papers, Library of Congress); Sheridan to General John Pope, July 22, 1874 (MS, Sheridan Papers, Library of Congress). Sherman had been promoted to lieutenant general.

[20] Sheridan to Pope, July 22, 1874.

[21] *Annual Report of the Commissioner of Indian Affairs, 1874,* 10, 214ff.

Promptly, General Augur sent all his available troops to the Texas border. On August 15 he joined Mackenzie's column moving from Fort Clark to Fort Concho, which they reached six days later. From here Augur must have gone on to Fort Griffin, for his instructions of August 28 to Mackenzie were written from that post. No doubt he had given Mackenzie his orders before the two men parted at Fort Concho, for the latter was well on his way to his old Fresh Water Fork base before Augur's written instructions of August 28 were ready.

In these instructions Augur stated that the object of the proposed campaign was to hunt out and defeat the waring Indians, and Mackenzie was to take such measures as necessary to accomplish that purpose. He warned that satisfactory results could not be gained in a day, "unless by great and unexpected good fortune," for the vast country to which the Indians had fled afforded "innumerable hiding places." Nor was Mackenzie to hesitate to cross reservation boundaries. *"You are at liberty to follow the Indians wherever they go, even to the Agencies,"* Augur wrote, but Mackenzie was to observe great care not to involve friendly reservation Indians. He also asked Mackenzie to impress on his subordinates that they should never for a moment relax in vigilance and precautions against surprise.

Augur's final suggestion related to Fort Griffin. "Supplies for your command will be sent to Fort Griffin," he stated, "until you suggest some other point." He urged him to designate the quantity and the time supplies should be at Fort Griffin to be hauled by his wagon trains moving westward.[22]

[22] William R. Hogan, "Special Report on Fort Griffin [Texas]" in Rister Papers (MS, Texas Technological College Library).

Satanta

Other troop columns were to help complete the squeeze on the warring Indians, to force them back to their reservations. Lieutenant Colonel George Buell was to operate from Fort Griffin with six companies of cavalry and two of infantry, under Mackenzie's direction. He was to march from Fort Griffin, across the Pease River to Red River, and then up that stream to the trail Mackenzie had made in 1872. He was to search for lurking Indians in the broken country between the Clear Fork and Red rivers.

Lieutenant Colonel John B. ("Black Jack") Davidson was to march westward from Fort Sill with six companies of cavalry, three of infantry, and forty-four Indian scouts. Colonel Nelson A. Miles would move southwesterly from Camp Supply, Indian Territory, with eight companies of cavalry, four of infantry, and three small field guns. And Major William Price was to advance from Fort Union, New Mexico, and down the Canadian River toward Antelope Hills, with four companies of cavalry. Thus almost three thousand cavalry and infantry, more blue-coated men than had ever before been used against Southern Plains Indians, would converge on these warring bands.

Mackenzie was on the march by August 23, starting with his "Southern Column" from the "Stone Ranch," sixteen miles up the North Concho from Fort Concho, for his old Fresh Water Fork base, the column now consisting of eight companies of the Fourth Cavalry, three of the Tenth Infantry, and one of the Eleventh Infantry. Additional infantry companies were added later.

By September 1, Mackenzie had reached the Fresh Water Fork of the Brazos (Catfish Creek), near the mouth of Blanco Canyon. Next day Second Lieutenant H. W. Lawton, quartermaster of the expedition and the Fourth

Cavalry's regimental quartermaster, started from Mackenzie's camp with empty wagons over the Mackenzie Trail for Fort Griffin, 140 miles away.

Augur admitted that the supply problem was serious; tons of forage must be hauled from Fort Griffin to Mackenzie's base, and from there to his cavalry troops scattered over the wind-swept plains. He sent his departmental quartermaster, General Samuel B. Holabird, to Dallas and other Texas towns "to see exactly what we can depend upon from the Contractors";[23] and he asked General Sheridan to send four thousand bushels of corn to Denison and Dallas, and from these towns to Camp Cooper, near Fort Griffin.

Meanwhile, Lawton's wagon trains were on the move, through all kinds of weather—dry northers and dust storms, rain, sleet, and snow. Wintry storms, the worst in the memory of Fort Griffin settlers, caused the loss of mules and much suffering to wagoners and soldiers escorting the trains, and delays on account of breakdowns or swollen rivers and creeks were common. Occasionally even uncommon road experiences added complications. On November 8, for example, Assistant Surgeon Rufus Choate reported the arrival of an empty train at Fort Griffin. Captain Hampson, in charge of its escort, had been thrown from his horse while he was chasing buffalo and had suffered serious injuries. He went to the post hospital for treatment.

Choate frequently reported in this month the arrival or departure of other trains. On December 10, Major Johnson, with Company G, Tenth Cavalry, left Griffin with a wagon train and traveled as far as the Clear Fork crossing,

[23] Augur to Sheridan, September 17, 1874 (MS, Sheridan Papers, Library of Congress).

where five mules were drowned in the high water and a wagon capsized and its contents lost. Another train, under the care of Lieutenant Burbank, remained nine wintry days pastured between Paint Creek and the Clear Fork because of high water; Lieutenant Gilbreath, with still another train, lost ten mules because of this storm. Choate reported that when Gilbreath met Burbank, the latter's mules had eaten all the forage of his train before he could get back to the post.[24]

But Mackenzie was on the move, forage or no forage. The rebellious Indians must be found and defeated. Winter had set in and he must wind up his campaign quickly, or else blizzards, sleet, and snow would pose dangerous handicaps.

After Mackenzie's troops had concentrated at his Fresh Water Fork base, the "Southern Column," now consisting of 450 enlisted men, 21 commissioned officers, and 3 acting assistant surgeons, on Sunday, September 20, moved up the canyon and out onto the Staked Plains, taking a course generally northward. From the night of September 24 until well into December, he and his troopers often faced cold northers, rain, mud, and snow. Moreover, wily Indians hovered on the column's flank, seeking to stampede the cavalry horses at night and skirmishing with the troopers to delay them. On fresh horses selected from their large "cavyyard" they were able to strike quickly and keep out of harm's way.

Their camps were difficult to find. Only *Comancheros* knew their hidden retreats. Among these was José Piedad Tafoya, whom the troopers captured. Mackenzie ordered

[24] "Medical History of the Post, Fort Griffin, Texas, 1867–81," as cited, 24–27, 30–31, 32, 34.

him to reveal the whereabouts of the main Indian camp, but he did not do so until he was hanged three times to a propped-up wagon tongue. Finally, half-strangled, he was willing to talk, and directed the scouts—Sergeant John B. Charlton, Chief Johnson, and Job, a Tonk warrior—to the Indian villages in the Palo Duro Canyon.[25] Mackenzie subsequently encountered two other *Comanchero* parties, but allowed them their freedom only to learn later that they had joined a large Indian war party moving eastward.

At daybreak, on September 27, 1874, Mackenzie's advance guard peered down the precipitous Palo Duro wall, east of the present village of Happy. Captain R. G. Carter later stated that the troopers could see the Indian lodges strung along the bottom of the canyon. Then the troopers moved down the canyon until they found a trail to descend. Here each officer and man had to dismount and lead his horse in single file down the narrow zig-zag path. At the steepest places, both men and horses slipped and slid, one by one, until they reached the bottom.[26]

Three troops had reached the canyon floor before the Indians, in their lodges asleep, awoke to discover them. Then pandemonium broke loose. Captain Eugene B. Beaumont's Troop A quickly re-formed and galloped after the fleeing Indians. On every hand the troopers saw buffalo robes, blankets, and miscellaneous Indian property strewn on the ground, as they dashed by abandoned village after village. The warriors had bolted up the precipitous canyon walls to escape as best they could. Many heavily laden

[25] Haley, *Fort Concho*, 220.
[26] Carter, *On the Border with Mackenzie*, 488; Mackenzie's Report in Augur's "Annual Report, 1874," as cited.

pack animals were running loose, while others stood tied to trees.

Mackenzie ordered troops D, I, and K to dismount and deploy as skirmishers across the canyon floor, and to keep up a lively long-range duel with the warriors farther up the canyon. This was done, Carter stated, to enable other troops to pull down lodges, chop up lodge poles, and pile up miscellaneous Indian belongings for huge bonfires.

Other troops re-forming in the canyon and running up it through the Indian's gauntlet of fire met Beaumont's troop driving down the canyon a large Indian pony herd which had been captured. By midafternoon the troopers had destroyed the Indian villages.

In the canyon, Mackenzie found himself in peril, for the Indians behind boulders and trees on either side of and high above his men put the troopers in an uncomfortable position. In addition, about noon Mackenzie saw a large number of warriors hastening down the canyon rim to occupy and block the trail down which his cavalry had descended to its present position. He promptly ordered Captain Gunther with Troop H to thwart this design. The result was a race between the two hostile forces, which the troopers won. Gunther not only drove back the foe but also screened Mackenzie's other troops ascending the canyon trail.[27]

Shortly Mackenzie re-formed his troops on the plains above the canyon by arranging them in a large hollow square, or living corral, about the captured horses. One

[27] Carter, *On the Border with Mackenzie,* 492; Mooney, "Calendar History of the Kiowas," *Seventeenth Annual Report of the Bureau of American Ethnology,* 1895–96, Part I, 210.

troop in battle line rode in front, one on each side, and one in the rear. In this manner they moved from the canyon for about twenty miles, until they reached Tule Canyon, where they bivouacked for the night. Next morning the scouts were permitted to select the best horses in the Indian herd, and then the rest were shot. Mackenzie did not intend to permit the Indians to recover their horses as they had done following the McClellan Creek fight in 1872.[28]

On October 1, 1874, Mackenzie reported briefly the results of the Palo Duro fight. He stated that he had captured and burned Comanche, Kiowa, and Cheyenne villages and supplies, and had taken and shot 1,048 ponies. His men had found only four dead warriors, although he did not know how many others the Indians had taken away from the field. The Indian women and children had escaped by climbing the cliffs above their villages and fleeing westward. Sergeant John B. Charlton reported that when he and Tonk scouts had ridden down the canyon, they had "passed over dead Indians everywhere."[29]

During the next few weeks Mackenzie's troopers constantly battled another formidable foe—bad weather—while by forced marches, following the elusive Indians, drenched for hour on hour by torrential rain, pierced by cold wind, and painfully slowed down by miry soil, they covered the plains between the Palo Duro and Blanco canyons. Their meandering trail in every sense was a *via mala,* for, in addition to these hardships, they suffered from fatigue and hunger because Lawton's supply wagons could

[28] "Annual Report, Department of Texas, 1874" (MS, Old Records Section, A. G. O., Division of War Records, National Archives, Washington); Miles, *Personal Recollections,* 174.

[29] In Augur's "Annual Report, 1874," as cited; R. G. Carter, *The Old Sergeant's Story* (New York, 1926), 109.

not always reach them. Only occasionally could one be pulled by double-team through the heavy mud. At last, Mackenzie sent his sick men and worn-out horses back to the Fresh Water base, to which he followed them on October 23.

Once again Mackenzie and his men could rest, sleep, and enjoy wholesome food, supplied from his Camp Cooper base. In addition, they performed routine duties, overhauled equipment, and shod their horses in preparation for a new expedition.

On October 31, Mackenzie learned that a large Indian village had been established on the head of the Double Mountain Fork of the Brazos, not far from present Post, Texas. He made preparations immediately to attack it. He would be supplied by wagon trains shuttling to and from Camp Cooper, although for present needs he would depend on pack mules. He regrouped his eight cavalry troops by leaving the sick men behind and taking only those who were physically fit. Twelve days' rations were issued to each troop, and by dusk he and his men rode hurriedly toward the southeast.

On November 2, a courier with mail from Fort Griffin overtook Mackenzie's column. Many of the men were dispirited because they had not heard from home or family for several weeks. Now that letters brought them encouraging news they could ride zestfully after the Indians. On November 5, Captain Carter entered in his log that a small Indian camp was struck near Tahoka Lake, "and a short, hot fight ensued in which four Indians were killed and 12 squaws, 7 papooses, and 156 ponies were captured."[30]

Mackenzie did not find the Double Mountain Fork In-

[30] Carter, *On the Border with Mackenzie,* 506.

dian village and returned to his supply base. "On the 11th," Carter reported, "our never-to-be-forgotten quartermaster, Lawton, left camp with a large train for Fort Griffin for more supplies—and by way of variety, on the 12th we had another 'norther' that double discounted the previous ones. Everybody stuck close to what shelter they had. For a couple of days we had some active drilling on foot, and meantime orders were issued for each company to prepare to start on the 16th on a 30-day scout; but on that day we had another severe wet 'norther,' making it impossible to move. For the next three days, rain, hail, sleet and snow alternated. There was one consolation, however, the Indians could not move any better than ourselves."[31]

Early in December, Mackenzie's cavalry and infantry, with all camp supplies were moved from the Fresh Water Fork base to Duck Creek, south of present Claremont, in Kent County, where Mackenzie had located a temporary supply base in 1871. His new change of base was made preparatory to breaking up the expedition. From here, a short time later, the cavalry and infantry units were sent to their respective posts—to Clark, McKavett and Concho, Griffin, and Richardson. Those companies marching to Griffin and Richardson had to travel eastward over the Mackenzie Trail of 1871 via the Double Mountain Fork of the Brazos, California, and Paint creeks, the Clear Fork of the Brazos, and Camp Cooper.

Previously, on December 3, Mackenzie and a part of his cavalry had left his Fresh Water Fork base to attack a large hostile Indian village reported to be near the head of Mucha Que, north of present Gail, in Borden County. Four days later, while nearing his quarry, a Lipan scout

[31] *Ibid.*, 507.

killed a Quahada vedette, and on the next day Lieutenant Lewis Warrington with a small detachment killed two other Comanches and captured a fifteen-year-old boy, named Vidot, who was later returned to his village near Fort Sill.[32]

Late that evening the troopers were again in the saddle, following an Indian trail toward Cedar Lake (Laguna Sabinas), sixty miles farther west, and about fourteen miles northwest of present Lamesa; but the Indians had abandoned this village before the cavalry could reach them. The troopers arrived about 11:00 A.M. the next day, and rested here several hours before they started their return journey. Mackenzie learned that the Quahadas had used this camping site and another at Laguna Quatro to pack buffalo meat preparatory to moving to the country "near the Río Grande above the mouth of the Pecos or to the Guadalupe Mountains."[33]

On December 19, Mackenzie and his tired troopers retraced their steps to the Duck Creek depot, where the Colonel found orders awaiting him to return to Fort Griffin. Wintry weather continued to plague him. He left Duck Creek on December 20, but he did not arrive at Griffin until eight days later on account of heavy rainfall, sleet, and snow.[34]

[32] Warrington to Acting Assistant Adjutant General, Scouting Expedition, December 19, 1874 (MS, 252–A. G. O., 1875, Division of War Records, National Archives, Washington).

[33] Mackenzie to Assistant Adjutant General, Department of Texas, January 7, 1875 (MS, Division of War Records, National Archives, Washington).

[34] For a previous assignment of Mackenzie cavalry and infantry companies, see, G. B. Russell to Mackenzie, December 5, 1874 (MS, Division of War Records, National Archives, Washington).

Although Lieutenant Colonel Buell had been nominally under the control of Mackenzie, he generally followed an independent course. He operated out of Fort Griffin and from a temporary supply base on Wanderer's Creek, in northwestern Texas, near the Red River. But he, too, encountered severe hardships in the form of rainy and wintry weather, and at one time was separated several days from his supply train because of high water. Yet he campaigned actively, moving up Red River, as originally planned, and then southward.

On October 9, 1874, he destroyed a large Kiowa village on the Salt Fork of the Brazos, twenty-six miles west of Double Mountain, killing eleven warriors and capturing fifty-six head of stock.[35] Later, he destroyed two other villages—one of seventy-five lodges and another of about one hundred—and drove their occupants helter-skelter out onto the Staked Plains, toward McClellan Creek.[36]

But winter was as severe on Buells troops as it was on Mackenzie's. In December he had to leave his frozen-in base in northwestern Texas and trek into Fort Griffin, because of "snow, rain, high streams, muddy roads, and cold weather."[37]

Davidson's, Miles', and Price's columns were also busy in the great Indian roundup. On September 12, 1874, Price's cavalry defeated a large Indian war party and drove it for several miles from the field. And while Davidson's column was moving west of Fort Sill, he was processing back to their agencies those defeated bands whose leaders recog-

[35] Sheridan, *Record of Engagements*, 42.

[36] "Medical History of the Post, Fort Griffin, Texas, 1867–81," as cited; "Post Returns, Fort Griffin, 1875" (MS, A. G. O., Division of War Records, Archives, Washington).

[37] Quoted in Haley, *Fort Concho*, 228–29.

122

nized the futility of further resistance. Miles continued to harass the fleeing warriors wherever they could be found. He also struck a large Indian war party in Wheeler County, Texas, on the Sweetwater, put it to flight, and captured a large quantity of supplies and equipment. On November 8, Captain Frank Baldwin of his command launched his famous wagon-train charge on a Cheyenne village on Mc-Clellan Creek, put the Indians to flight, and recaptured two of the German sisters, Adelaide and Julia.[38] The two older sisters—Catharine and Sophia—still remained captives.

By the spring of 1875, the war bands were defeated; their villages, supplies, and horses were captured. Even during the preceding fall, Agent John D. Miles wrote, small war parties continued to arrive at the agency to surrender, but that it was not until March, 1875, that "the main Cheyenne village under Gray Beard, Heap o' Birds, Stone Calf, Bull Bear and minor chiefs surrendered to General Neil a short distance from the agency [Darlington], and were promptly disarmed and placed under guard, and their ponies confiscated and sold."[39] He said that it would be difficult to imagine a more wretched and poverty-stricken community than these people presented after they were placed in prison camps, a statement equally true for Comanche and Kiowa returnees.

Through the aid of Catharine and Sophia German, who were recovered when the main Cheyenne village surrendered, army officers identified the Cheyenne war leaders. In all, thirty-two men and one woman were arrested

---

[38] Alice Blackwood Baldwin, *Memoirs of Major General Frank D. Baldwin* (Los Angeles, 1929), 70ff.

[39] *Annual Report of the Commissioner of Indian Affairs, 1875* (Washington, 1875), 269.

and added to a party of nine Comanches and twenty-six Kiowas to be sent to St. Augustine, Florida, for confinement. Agent Haworth stated that among the Kiowas exiled were two of the most prominent chiefs, Lone Wolf and Swan, and that among the lesser chiefs were Double Vision, Woman's Heart, and White Horse. Yet, White Horse had gained great notoriety by reckless, daring acts of raiding.[40]

This much-dreaded, severe punishment of hostile leaders brought to an end the long period of "moonlight raids." Settlers of Western Texas could now turn to their domestic problems without fear of the raider's scalping knife.

[40] *Ibid.*, 272.

VII The Rampageous Flat

W HILE BUELL'S and Mackenzie's troopers were corralling the Staked Plains Indians, and their wagon trains were shuttling back and forth between Fort Griffin and their supply bases, Fort Griffin life was drab and routine—drill, reveille, guard mount, retreat, tatoo, flag raising and lowering, and occasional inspections.

Such monotony brought delinquencies and infractions of military regulations. Frequent desertions of enlisted men, and sometimes of low-rank officers, occurred; on one occasion the baker deserted and the bakery could not be used, for no one else knew his art. As previously mentioned, six enlisted men were quartered in each small one-room picket hut, and as a consequence they suffered from a lack of ventilation; those in tents during winter months had "no means of heating except from kettles or pans of hot coals." The latter were not only inadequate but fire hazards as well. Assistant Surgeon Henry McElderry recommended to the post commander the building of more picket huts with shingled roofs, "properly raised, floored and braced," but they were not provided. Under such conditions, it is not surprising that enlisted men occasionally flaunted military decorum.

There were frequent riots, drunken debauches, fisticuffs, and more serious fights with weapons, and hospital attendants had to treat many patients for "contusions," particularly when brawls occurred between Negro and white soldiers, or between Negro soldiers and civilians.

In December, 1874, Assistant Surgeon D. G. Caldwell reported that "fully one-half of the surgical cases occurring in times of peace" were produced through whiskey, and that most of the whiskey provided troops in a garrison was supplied by sutlers. He said that recently a comfortable school-library building had been erected and put in use at the post. It reduced drunkenness, for soldiers employed their spare time with "good readable novels," rather than with whiskey.[1]

Don Biggers wrote than on one occasion a Negro cowboy, generally known as "Old Dick," came to town and started a civil war. At once he proceeded to get drunk, got on his horse and rode into the lower part of town, and threatened to make real trouble. John Birdwell, the town marshal, organized a posse of four or five men and went down to arrest him. But "Old Dick" was not ready for the calaboose; he learned of their coming and moved off into a near-by mesquite thicket.

"Old Dick" was on his horse, the posse on foot, but the posse found him and the battle started. While "Old Dick" was wheeling his horse about, however, he accidentally shot it in the back of the head, killing it instantly. On foot he was no match for his attackers, who literally shot him

---

[1] "Medical History of the Post, Fort Griffin, Texas, 1867–81," as cited, 34. See in particular the entry for December 31, 1874.

to pieces, one shot passing from jaw to jaw severing his tongue. Birdwell reported back to Justice of the Peace J. P. Steele that he could find "a dead Negro down there in the mesquites." Steele sent other men at once with a discarded door to bring him in. "Old Dick" was taken to an elderly Negro woman's house and placed on a pile of shucks to die, and a guard of one or two men was left with him. But to everyone's amazement, he did not die. Next morning Dr. J. L. Powell, post assistant surgeon, cleaned and dressed his wounds, and stitched his tongue. "Old Dick" refused chloroform, indicating to Powell that the needle would not hurt him. The Negress served as his nurse and he recovered. One night a party of men rode into town and took him to a ranch on the Salt Fork of the Brazos.[2]

McElderry also listed routine matters, even weather phenomena. On July 10, 1870, he mentioned the fall of 6.90 inches of rain in five hours, which caused overflows in Collins Creek and the Clear Fork; on February 23, 1873, he reported that "Troops of the Command were excused from drill, . . . because of a *severe dust storm*."[3]

Assistant Surgeon Carlos Carvallo at the Fort Griffin hospital in 1872 explained that the military personnel called the settlement below Government Hill the "Bottom" or the "Flat";[4] within five years it had grown from a few squatter houses to a boisterous, bustling village. Its main street extended from the foot of the hill to the Clear Fork,

[2] Biggers, *Shackelford County Sketches;* see section entitled "Fort Griffin." Fuller details are found in a letter, J. G. Kenan to Etta Soule, February 15, 1947 (MS in Soule Papers–Robert Nail Collection, Albany, Texas).

[3] "Medical History of the Post, Fort Griffin, Texas, 1867–81," as cited, 178, 253.

[4] *Ibid.*, 266.

along which, on either side, were a few gambling dives and eating places.

Among the early Main Street businessmen was Sam Newcomb, who had already run the gamut of border hardships, Indian danger, and deprivations while serving as a surveyor in Stephens County and teaching a subscription school at Fort Davis, farther down the Clear Fork. In 1867, Newcomb and his heroic and resourceful wife and child had settled on Collins Creek above the fort, and Newcomb had established a mercantile business in the Flat, just below Government Hill.[5]

By 1871, the village had become the only trading point for the upper Clear Fork settlers, who for the most part were ranchers. George Greer's and J. C. Lynch's holdings were on the Hubbard, about twenty-five miles southeast of Fort Griffin; Joe Browning's place was below Fort Davis on the Clear Fork, and farther up the river were those of Uncle Joe Matthews and W. H. Ledbetter. Then, above Fort Griffin, John Larn located near the confluence of Tecumseh Creek and the Clear Fork; Mart Hoover was temporarily at the Old Stone Ranch on Walnut Creek, and Judge C. K. Stribling was in the Lamb's Head Valley.

A short time later drifters—bullwhackers, cowpunchers, gamblers, toughs, and prostitutes—came to the Flat to fleece the unsuspecting and to ply their unholy trades. There were personal privileges aplenty and no legal restraints. Saloons thrived and gambling was lucrative. In front of every store, saloon, and business house was a long hitching rack, which was generally lined with saddled horses, and the street was congested and jammed with ox- or mule-drawn wagons and horse-drawn hacks and bug-

[5] Matthews, *Interwoven*, 53.

gies. To attract the liquor-buying and adventurous visitors, pianos, fiddles, banjos, and guitars ground out their lilting tunes, and scantily attired Cyprians walked the streets to add their allurements.[6] But the music was marred by a babel of boisterous talk, whoops, curses, and hoarse laughter. It was not uncommon to see Tonkawa Indians, both men and women, in a state of beastly intoxication, rendering it unsafe even for Fort Griffin officers and enlisted men to go down to the Flat unarmed, as the Tonks and white toughs had bowie knives and firearms about them.

Writing in 1874, Rufus Choate, then assistant surgeon of Fort Griffin, said that the Flat had experienced its first crime wave two years previously. Commander W. H. Wood of the Eleventh Infantry had become concerned about increasing outlawry and had acted promptly to eradicate it. He had declared that the Flat and the surrounding area were within the government reservation, and ordered transient gamblers, outlaws, and women to leave, an order they promptly obeyed. Then, Choate reported, "the low whiskey shops and gambling-halls of the flat were weeded out."[7]

Among those who left was a barkeeper named Peppert (alias "Joe Bowers"), but for another reason. The Assistant Surgeon wrote that he was a "desperate and noted desperado" who had already murdered two men in cold blood "within sight of the waving Stars and Stripes without any effort being taken by the military authorities to bring him to justice."

Bowers had carried on a feud with another character

[6] "Frontier Life of Uncle Joe S. McCombs," in J. R. Webb Papers (MS, R. N. Richardson Collection, Hardin-Simmons University).

[7] "Medical History of the Post, Fort Griffin, Texas, 1867–81," as cited, 25. See entry for November 8, 1874.

named J. B. Cockrell, whom Bowers had attempted three times to kill. First Bowers had killed a horse under Cockrell; second, he had inflicted "a severe and dangerous wound," for which Cockrell was treated in the post hospital from February 18, to March 2, 1872.[8] Doubtless the treatment of Cockrell and undesirable civilians in the post hospital caused the Assistant Surgeon to criticize Commander Wood for his policy. He named nine men, including Cockrell, who should not have had this service: Denis Dotson, John Krause, Mortimer Stanley, Henry Dunn, John Bright, J. B. Cockrell, and Florentine Valdez, all of whom paid less than they would have paid for board "in the 'Flat' or 'Bottom.'" He estimated that government losses ranged all the way from $2.50 on Sims, who was in the hospital for five days, to $35.00 on Dotson's stay of seventy days. From July 9, 1873, to January 1, 1874, he could better justify medical aid to James Shackelford, who was in the hospital, suffering from a rattlesnake bite.[9]

As soon as Cockrell had recovered, he went gunning for Bowers. But a "third time" had its charm for Bowers; on May 3, 1872, he killed Cockrell.

Henry Griswold Comstock later gave the details of the Bowers-Cockrell feud, although he remembered Cockrell as "Corcoran." He said that Bowers was the most pros-

[8] *Ibid.*, 266. See entry for May 22, 1872.

[9] *The Frontier Echo*, August 23, 1878, gave the following "Cure for Rattlesnake Bite," for many people in the Fort Griffin country during the spring and summer were in need of an effective remedy: "Apply a plaster of coal oil and saleratus to the wound, and bandage the limb tightly between the wound and body. In the meantime give the patient as much sweet milk as he can possibly take. Keep the plaster moist by pouring coal oil on the cloth without removing it from the wound. Keep up the treatment until the inflammation is entirely allayed."

perous of the three saloonkeepers in the Flat,[10] his saloon and gambling place being located fifty feet north of York's store, near the upper end of Main Street. After he had had his horse shot from under him, Cockrell had lost money at cards to Bowers' right-hand gambler, John Murphy, and a pistol duel had resulted. The fight started in the saloon, and Cockrell was hit two or three times before he and his friends ran outside and found protection behind a pile of post-oak posts, fifty or sixty feet away. From this vantage point, for a short time the besieged men kept up the battle with Bowers and Murphy, but without fatal consequences. Finally, Cockrell broke off the fight without further injury, and went to the Fort Griffin hospital where his wounds were treated, as has been related.

After this affair, he became a habitué of the other two saloons, in one of which he boasted while drunk that he was out to get Bowers. A listener brought this disquieting news to the intended victim, who arranged with the gossip-monger to keep him informed of Cockrell's new hanging-out places. While searching for them, he was to carry over his shoulder a stick with a red handkerchief attached to the upper end, which he was to lower when he found Cockrell.

Watching his ferret from his own saloon, Bowers saw him dip his flag before the door of the nearest saloon. He immediately seized his double-barreled shotgun, hurried down the street and into the saloon, and emptied both barrels into Cockrell's breast. Then he returned to his own establishment. Later, when he was told that the sheriff was after him, he arranged with Murphy to manage the saloon and prepared to leave, for he did not wish to risk a trial.

[10] Comstock to J. R. Webb, August 26, 1952.

The local peace officer was slow to arrest him; he was permitted to go at large for a few days and even to visit the post.[11] He had previously killed a Negro, John Carter, a Fort Griffin wood contractor, for which crime he had been arrested and tried, but acquitted. But now, fearing conviction on a second charge of murder, he hurriedly rode down the Clear Fork valley to escape.

Comstock had recently located on King's Creek, about twenty miles east of Griffin, on the mail route between Fort Smith, Arkansas, and Fort Concho, Texas. At this time he was building a picket house, by cutting posts eight or nine feet long and seven or eight inches in diameter and setting them vertically in a boxed trench which he had dug for his floor plan. He was interrupted in his work by the voice of a horseman who came riding out of a near-by thicket. The horseman was Bowers. He asked Comstock what he was doing, looked over his work critically, and was reported to have said: "Why! that is a work of art! You must be an artist!" He added that he was running from the law and could not tarry, then he rode away through the timbers.

The Flat's first crime wave was ended by Wood's prompt measures; the unsavory characters closed the doors of their resorts and moved out. But many others soon came to take their places.

From 1875 to 1880, the Flat increased in size two-fold, growing to a town of about one thousand persons, with perhaps twice that many transients, including buffalo hunters and cowboys. Here the revolver settled more differences among men than the judge, and straight shooting could promise long life more than could fresh air and sunshine.

[11] "Medical History of the Post, Fort Griffin, Texas, 1867–81," as cited. See entry for May, 1872.

Fort Griffin soldiers were frequently implicated in these affrays. A news release of October 26, 1875, reported "a slight unpleasantness" between soldiers and citizens, which for a time made things quite lively. A local observer said that "several shots were fired and a few persons hit but none seriously wounded. Some threats of burning the town were made, but up to 10:00 P.M. everything was quiet. . . . Old grudges are said to be the causes of the rumpus."[12]

Relations between the citizens and soldiers remained strained for many months, especially between white ruffians and Negro soldiers. This unhappy condition may have led to the occasion in October, 1876, when a buffalo hunter went on a spree after "tanking up" on whiskey and attempted to become a one-man army to rid Fort Griffin of its Negro soldiers. He staggered up Government Hill to "run all them d—— Yankees out of the mess hall." The unsuspecting Negro soldiers were at supper when he arrived. Brandishing a pistol, he ordered them to rise from their tables and back out of the door, one at a time. While he was shooting over their heads, they shot out of the door! When the last one was out, the crusader warned them that the first one who put his head back in the door would "get it shot off."

The troopers hardly needed this admonition, for they were on the move. They informed their captain that a wild man was running amuck, and the captain in turn, ordered Lieutenant Jouett to proceed to the mess hall with a firing squad.

---

[12] *Denison Daily News,* October 27, 1875. A telegraph line had been completed to Fort Griffin some time previously, which gave the state and nation a daily news coverage from Fort Griffin.

The sheriff also heard about the buffalo hunter's rampage and promptly went to the mess hall and arrested him. He took him to a vacant shack in the Flat to sleep off his drunk, and propped a log against the door to keep him in. But the day was cold and the buffalo hunter did not sleep; instead, he tore up the floor and used its timbers to build a fire, which presently became too warm—the shack was in flames. The sheriff returned to the burning building just in time to drag his coughing and sputtering prisoner out. It was not necessary for him to use other sobering means, for the smoke and fire had restored the drunk man's senses.[13]

The Flat's night life furnished a local correspondent good copy for the *Frontier Echo* of Jacksboro, Texas. On one occasion he wrote: "Cowboys raising hell in town last night. Marshall William C. Gilson put a load of buckshot in the chest and arm of William Harpe, though he was not seriously hurt." Other reports were equally lurid. "Hoss Inghram paid a $1.00 fine for being drunk. . . . A row occurred in the saloon last Saturday night but no one was hurt, although six-shooters and chairs were flourished."[14]

Tenants of the "red light" district also took the spotlight. These women were often before the Justice's court either to testify about saloon and street brawls or to pay fines because of their vulgar language in public places. Local authorities did not drive them from town or close their houses; instead they required them to pay each year a $100 fine, thereby virtually licensing them. If the offender was arraigned for running a disorderly house, she would plead guilty and pay a fine of $100. Then the officer

[13] Grant, "The Early History of Shackelford County," as cited, 77–78.
[14] *Frontier Echo* (Jacksboro, Texas), November 19, 23, and December 14, 1877.

would not arrest her again during that year unless she committed another kind of offense. Examples of this practice are found in such news items as "State vs. Lottie Deno. Running disorderly house. Pleaded guilty, fined $100.00 and cost. . . . State vs. Mollie McCabe. Keeping disorderly house. Pleaded guilty, fined $100.00 and cost."[15]

Sinful Mollie had previously met with another misfortune. The *Frontier Echo* of November 19, 1875, reported thus: "Last Friday night a fire broke out in Mollie McCabe's 'Place of Beautiful Sin.' She owned the building which was entirely consumed, together with her household goods and clothes. The fire was caused by one of the damsels of spotted virtue."

Edgar Rye later wrote that among the wild, daredevil characters who frequented the resorts of the Flat "was a female monstrosity known as Lottie Deno."[16] Yet she could play the role of a lady, nurtured in refined society and of gentle birth. At Griffin, however, she belonged to the gambling fraternity and at one time operated a disorderly house. Otherwise, Lottie kept herself aloof from the open debauchery and depravity of the other lewd women about her.

Lottie arrived one evening in 1876 on the Jacksboro stage, riding on top of the coach beside the driver, Dick Wheeler. And from then until her departure, she was secluded in her little Clear Fork shanty, except when she visited stores to make needed purchases, or when she, night after night, played cards or presided over the Bee Hive Saloon's gambling room.

Because of Lottie's aloofness and air of mystery, many

[15] *Fort Griffin Echo,* March 24, 1880.
[16] Rye, *The Quirt and the Spur,* 70–71.

rumors about her identity were current. Edgar Rye thought that she lived the dual life of a saint in the East and a desperate character in the West, and another reporter claimed that she was a New Orleans philanthropist. Still others chose to believe that she was the daughter of an aristocratic Southern family, whose prestige and fortune had fallen with the Confederate cause,[17] and that she had turned to gambling to recoup her fortune. At Griffin, she kept her past a secret; she remained a recluse, refusing to receive visitors, male or female. But in the gambling hall she saw many a brawl, heard the violent oaths of drunken and depraved men, witnessed gun battles, and "when the smoke cleared away there were dead men lying in pools of blood near the card tables."[18]

Lottie was unquestionably an attractive woman, of medium size, shapely, with an abundance of dark red hair and sparkling black eyes. She was always well dressed and walked with the air of a perfect lady.

Henry Herron, who was deputy sheriff during Lottie's stay at the Flat, said that she frequented the gambling halls but not the saloons, "and if she ever took a drink, I never saw it. However, I do know that she had the name in the underworld of being a kept woman, and that her keeper was a prominent saloon keeper, a married man whose name I will not mention." His saloon was the Bee Hive, over the door of which was a swinging sign a traveling artist had drawn. It showed a beehive festooned with honeysuckle,

[17] J. Marvin Hunter, "The Lottie Deno I Knew," *West Texas Historical Association Year Book*, Vol. XXIII (October, 1947), 30.

[18] Rye, *The Quirt and the Spur*, 71; Henry Herron later stated that "walking from the gambling hall to her house was her only appearance on the street." See "Early History Notes," in J. R. Webb Papers (MS, R. N. Richardson Collection, Hardin-Simmons University).

about which were swarming bees. Under the hive was this bit of verse:

> *In this hive we are all alive,*
> *Good whiskey makes us funny;*
> *If you are dry step in and try*
> *The flavor of our honey.*

One day a twenty-two-year-old nice-looking Illinois lad, Johnny Golden, came to town, "and Lottie fell for him and quit the saloonkeeper." This led to Johnny's death. A contemporary concluded that the saloonkeeper could tolerate neither a rival nor loss of face.

Here is what happened. Johnny was arrested by two local officers, who claimed that they had a warrant for his arrest for horse stealing. Johnny protested that he had never owned a horse, but the officers marched him away toward the Fort Griffin guardhouse, although the town calaboose was only about twenty yards away. They never reached the guardhouse, and the officers reported that a mob had taken their prisoner and killed him.[19] It was rumored in the underworld, however, that the saloonkeeper had paid the officers $250 to dispose of him. Johnny's body was found back of Hank Smith's wagon yard, only about two blocks from Shaughnessy's saloon, where he had been arrested.[20] No investigation of the affair was ever made.

A few days later Lottie left on the Jacksboro stage, al-

[19] Henry Herron's "Recollections and Experiences of Frontier Life" as told to J. R. Webb, July 17, 1940, in J. R. Webb Papers (MS, R. N. Richardson Collection, Hardin-Simmons University). James W. Stell, a buffalo hunter, stated to the author on March 3, 1929, that "I seen him [a local officer] . . . kill John Golding [Golden] in the middle of the street."

[20] Herron's "Recollections and Experiences of Frontier Life," as cited.

though it has been reported that her departure was not general knowledge for a few days. When the sheriff and other Griffinites entered her shack in search of her, they found it nicely furnished. On her bedspread was pinned a note, reading: "Sell this outfit and give the money to someone in need of assistance."[21]

Temporarily, at least, Lottie next settled in Jacksboro. Mrs. Ida L. Huckabay states that her grandmother knew Lottie here and thought she was a kind-hearted woman, which was the consensus of others who knew her.[22] Just how long she remained in Jacksboro is not a matter of record.

The late O. W. Williams, who in the 1870's was a land locater and South Plains surveyor, was in and out of Fort Griffin, but did not know Lottie Deno there, although he did say, however, that the Flat was a "tough old Fort." In 1879, he went to New Mexico on a two-year hitch as a mining prospector, and three years later he was postmaster at Silver City and also deputy clerk of the federal court. Here he learned of, but never met, Lottie, who, now going by another name, operated a restaurant. She had married a notorious local gambler and saloon man. After her husband's death, she joined the Episcopal church and became well known for her social welfare work.[23] When she died in Deming about 1934, reportedly at the age of eighty, New Mexico newspapers carried lengthy stories about her charitable activities.

There were also other "soiled ladies" called to appear

[21] Rye, *The Quirt and the Spur*, 74.

[22] Mrs. Ida L. Huckaby to Carl Coke Rister, July 16, 1954. See also Ida L. Huckaby, *Ninety-four Years in Jack County, 1854–1948* (Jacksboro, 1949), 155.

[23] O. W. Williams to Carl Coke Rister, November 2, 1935.

before the Shackelford County Commissioners' Court. On November 4, 1876, "Long Kate" and "Minnie" were tried for fighting in a grocery store, and others were tried for operating disorderly houses, or for profanity and card playing. The names of male offenders also appear in the court's records. One case was the "State of Texas *vs.* Lynch, Curly, and Hurricane Bill" for "playing cards in a saloon." This case was dismissed on November 13, 1876. Well may the reader wonder why the commissioners tried this case and others of a similar nature since gambling went on day and night in the Flat's saloons.[24]

Still, Fort Griffin and the Flat enjoyed more wholesome fun and frolic—picnics, singings, stage plays by local talent, and horse racing. Pete Haverty was an active promoter of racing. He kept a race horse, a paint, which had a reputation of outrunning anything in the country. By word-of-mouth or published advertisement, he frequently challenged any ambitious sportsman to match his race horse with his own. In one issue of the *Fort Griffin Echo* he ran this notice: "Pete Haverty, Livery, Feed and Stage Stable. Will Swap or Run Horses with any Man."[25]

A short time later, his challenge was accepted. A stranger came along driving a grizzled gray to a buggy. The horse seemed to be anything else but a racer; it looked as if calves had chewed off its mane and tail, and it was gaunt and flea-bitten, seemingly without ambition for speed competition. To the amazement of local sportsmen, however, the stranger matched his horse against Haverty's and also took a number of side bets, which Haverty and

[24] Haverty published this challenge in the *Fort Griffin Echo* as late as July 17, 1878.
[25] Herron's "Recollections and Experiences of Frontier Life" as cited.

the sharpers eagerly offered. The race presented little competition; Haverty's horse was beaten to a frazzle. The newcomer cleaned Haverty of $500 and collected a considerable amount from the others, and then quietly went on his way seeking other profitable fields, for no other races could be staged along the Clear Fork.[26]

Occasionally, Editor G. W. Robson, at Jacksboro, devoted space in his *Frontier Echo* to men and women violating the law, not even excluding peace officers. On October 4, 1878, he captioned an article, "Murder at Griffin." On the previous night, Robson stated, Henry Cruger, brother of Sheriff Cruger of Shackelford County, and June Leach, quartermaster's clerk known to many Griffin citizens, and several others were playing pool. When Leach accidentally stepped on Cruger's foot, the latter said, "If you step on my foot again, I will knock the stuffins out of you." Leach assured him it was an accident and begged his pardon, but coolly added that as to "knocking the stuffins out," he did not believe Cruger could do it.

"As to the remainder of the difficulty," Robson wrote, "reports conflict; one being that Cruger immediately drew a pistol and shot Leach; another, that Leach knocked Cruger down with his fist and picked up a chair with which to strike him, when Cruger raised up, drew his pistol and fired with fatal effect. Leach died Saturday forenoon. Cruger was arrested, and after hearing the testimony, the justice admitted him to bail in the sum of $2,000, which was readily given." Cruger was never convicted of the crime.

[26] "Henry Herron," MS in J. R. Webb papers, as previously cited.

VIII Cowboys, Outlaws, and Vigilantes

B<small>Y THE LATE</small> 1870's the dawn of civilization had crept up the Clear Fork Valley, which Jesse Stem, Randolph B. Marcy, Robert S. Neighbors, and Robert E. Lee had earlier known. This sylvan paradise was subject to kaleidoscopic changes—from its dazzling snow field of midwinter to its choking dust storm of March, and from its flower-splashed landscape of May to the sun-baked and withered land of August.

It was still the home of wild life: the panther, the lobo, the coyote, the buffalo, and such game birds as the turkey and quail. Through its grassy carpet crawled the venomous diamondback rattlesnake, the tarantula, scorpion, and spider—all the enemies of humankind. And here dwelt other dangerous creatures of human form. In this Eden was planted one of the West's wildest towns, the festering center of bestiality, crime, and murder.

Nevertheless, this was a beautiful land, too beautiful and potential, indeed, for rugged cowmen to ignore. The Matthews and Reynolds families, who had earlier found here a dangerous but inviting frontier, now expanded their

141

holdings, built substantial stone houses, and pre-empted the state's domain to graze their herds, like the herders of olden times. Mart V. Hoover and his young bride moved northeastward from the Old Stone Ranch about two and one-half miles and built a neat new structure on the south side of the winding Clear Fork, with the river almost fencing in their back yard, and with an undulating prairie forming a pleasing front view. About one-half mile farther north and across the river, near its great bend, stood the stately home of George Reynolds, in whose body was yet an arrowhead of a foe with whom he had warred for this land. The house was on a high plateau, which gave its occupants a commanding view of the surrounding country.

In January, 1876, Barber Watkins Reynolds had built an equally fine house about one-half mile farther down the river. Here on December 25 of that year, Sallie Reynolds, the future author of the family history, *Interwoven,* married John Alexander Matthews.[1] This place was later known as "Reynolds Bend Shrine." Still farther down the river N. L. and Susan Bartholomew built an attractive New England design, two-story house, within easy reach of their up-river neighbors. It stood at the foot of mesquite-clad hills, with fine pecans growing along the meandering Clear Fork, about half a mile away, like a giant hedge enclosing a jumbo front lawn.

[1] Thomas Lindsay Blanton, *Pictorial Supplement to Interwoven* (Albany, Texas, 1953), 31. Judge Blanton was connected with one of the "interwoven" families. He married May Louise Matthews on September 27, 1900. He was a graduate in law from the University of Texas and a district judge for eight years, 1909–16, and then was elected to Congress from the Jumbo District, embracing fifty-nine counties running from El Paso to Mineral Wells. He served with distinction in the United States Congress for twenty years.

Farther eastward and on the north side of the Clear Fork, D. C. Campbell built a frame house in 1877. He was to become in later years the secretary-treasurer of the Reynolds Cattle Company. One-half mile below him on the same side of the river, the W. D. Reynolds residence was erected four or five years later.

Twenty-five or more miles up the Clear Fork, on Miller Creek in Baylor County, and on Tonkawa Creek in Stonewall County, other adventurous ranchers had gone to stake out their claims within what was previously almost an untouched frontier. In May, 1873, Emmett Roberts built a dugout near the Clear Fork, just below present-day Nugent.[2] He and his cowboys had to divide their time each day between attending their cattle and keeping a watch for marauding Comanches and Kiowas. Living just as hazardously were their neighbors, Mode and C. J. Johnson, who had pre-empted a fine ranch site on Chimney Creek, about five miles away. On Tonkaway Creek, in Stonewall County, was John Goff's range. He had entered this rugged country in the winter of 1873. In the following year in the same area, one-armed Jim Reed had built a pretentious stone house to serve both as headquarters and fort, since hostile Indians yet claimed this country as their own. North of Fort Griffin, in Baylor County, was located the Millett Ranch, which the *Echo* of June 21, 1879, described as "one of the toughest spots this side of hell."

This patternized map of Clear Fork country ranches and periphery holdings was but a segment of the settlement extending along the entire Texas frontier, from the Red River to the Río Grande. These ranchers composed the vanguard

[2] "Frontier Experiences of Emmett Roberts of Nugent, Texas," *West Texas Historical Association Year Book*, Vol. III (June, 1927), 43, 44.

of a culture which would soon transform that country. J. Wright Mooar, a notable Southern Plains buffalo hunter, has well said that as the hide hunters drove the Indians and buffalo back, "the cowman, ever quick and alert to see opportunity, followed in the wake . . . so closely that many large herds were located within hearing of the roar of the Big Fifty."[3] In later years each succeeding zone occupied by pre-empting cattlemen was to move westward as land-hungry farmers came in to establish their 160-acre claims.

Griffin, or the Flat, also benefited by this westward surge of immigrants, particularly when the cowboys, surveyors, buffalo hunters, and teamsters came to town. Both the rising cattle and buffalo-hide industries, pouring an ever increasing stream of commercial wealth into the town, indirectly engendered the Flat's turbulence and outlawry. The Flat's population was heterogeneous. Soldiers and Indians had come by direction of the federal government; wide-awake businessmen, to find opportunity for profit; gamblers, to harvest an inviting field; outlaws and absconders, for a refuge of safety; the ever present cowboys, to find surcease from the trail, or to buy liquor and to seek entertainment; and the buffalo hunters, to sell "flint" hides and purchase supplies.

The opening of the Western Cattle Trail, starting from the vicinity of San Antonio and running northward, presented Griffinites with not only glittering commercial opportunities, but also a highly dangerous problem of law and order. By 1875 the Kansas farmers' frontier, moving from east to west, had overrun the Chisholm Trail at

[3] Don H. Biggers, *From Cattle Range to Cotton Patch* (Bandera, Texas, 1944), 48; "Frontier Experiences of J. Wright Mooar," *West Texas Historical Association Year Book*, Vol. IV (June, 1928), 91.

Courtesy Watt Matthews

Frank Conrad

Courtesy Mrs. E. Matthews Casey

Joe B. Matthews

points and had caused many Texas cattlemen to seek a new route farther west for their cattle drives to Kansas markets.

Seeing an opportunity to tap the Chisholm Trail, Griffin merchants sent a clever agent to Belton to intercept the cattle drivers of spring and summer and to persuade them to point their cattle up the Leon River and thence northward via Fort Griffin. By this approach they could intersect the Western Trail from San Antonio to Dodge City, a southwestern terminus town and a lively market for cattle on the Santa Fe railroad. Many cattle drivers accepted the suggestion, much to the chagrin of Fort Worth merchants, who heretofore had enjoyed an exclusive trade with those cowmen following the Chisholm Trail.[4]

Griffin businessmen chortled with glee. Now they had the advantage of Fort Worth merchants, which they would exploit to the limit. Griffin was on the boom. Early and late they spared no effort to welcome the dusty trail drivers and to show them every courtesy.

A Griffin reporter for the *Fort Worth Democrat,* writing under the pseudonym "Lone Star," literally exuded his town's new spirit. In April, 1876, he informed envious Fort Worth readers that southern Texas cattle were coming in rapidly, and that the driving season's total over the Western Trail should reach 125,000 head. He stressed the fact that these cattle drives to Dodge City were moving from southern Texas via Griffin and Cantonment, Indian Territory.[5] Other reports prove that his estimate of the annual drive

[4] Wayne Gard, *The Chisholm Trail* (Norman, 1954), 227–28; P. W. Reynolds to J. R. Webb, January 21, 1947 (MS in J. R. Webb Papers–R. N. Richardson Collection, Hardin-Simmons University).

[5] *Fort Worth Democrat,* April 22, 1876.

was not far wrong. The *Jacksboro Frontier Echo* of July 21, 1876, stated that 73,000 cattle had already passed Griffin, bound for Dodge City.

The shaded valley of the Clear Fork was a desirable camping ground for the trail drivers. Here they could find rest and range for their cattle and much-needed supplies and boisterous entertainment for themselves.

Cowboys for trail driving were scarce, and often a cowman must employ any rider whom he could pick up without asking about his antecedents. For this reason some of the cowboys visiting the Flat were desperadoes and murderers, ready for any kind of violence, and their readiness to engage in shootings, knifings, and bawdy-house brawls added to Griffin's bedlam and chaos. Other cowboys, more inclined to fun than violence, rode into town to "let off steam" by firing six-shooters recklessly. They meant no great harm; they only sought release for their pent-up spirits, to compensate for their tedium during many days of trail driving.

Griffin had been a resort for outlaws and scoundrels since the early 1870's, and it was a place which the incoming cowboys now found surprisingly tough. Within a period of twelve years, thirty-five men had been "publicly killed," eight or ten others found dead, and officers of the law and the vigilantes had shot or strung up twelve more. So emigrant cowboy "bad men" had no trouble finding dangerous antagonists—cold-eyed killers, or crooked dealers of faro, monte, and poker.

Even the name of Collins Creek was significant. It had gained its name during pre–Fort Griffin days when a "Mr. Collins" was killed there, presumably by the "Old Law Mob" or "O. L. M." No one knows just what charges the "Mob" could have justly brought against him, if indeed its members cared.[6] And after Fort Griffin was established, killings below Government Hill mounted, as may be seen from a tabulation made later.

In 1870, a rancher and a cowboy had quarreled over a wage disagreement. When a fight was imminent, a mutual friend had stepped between the two angry men to arbitrate the matter and lost his life. The notorious Bowers, previously mentioned, had also murdered two men. But perhaps the most callous murderer was a drunken outlaw, who had shot a harmless old Tonk because he got in his way. The killer was put in the town calaboose until he sobered up, and then allowed to go his way.

On another occasion a cowboy rode into town, hitched his horse in front of a saloon, and went in for a drink. He got drunk and left his horse tied all day to the hitching rack. His boss learned of the neglect of the horse and came for him. As he was leading the animal away, the cowboy saw him and demanded that he drop the reins. When he refused, the cowboy shot him to death.

Still another killing had involved peace officers. The sheriff and a deputy had sought to arrest a man named Hampton, who was walking across the street directly toward them. He made no move to throw up his hands when he was ordered to do so, perhaps because, as was learned later, he was partially deaf. The deputy began shooting, and when he had emptied his gun, Hampton fell dead. Subsequently, the deputy was reported to have offered a wager that the bullet holes in the man's body could be covered with a silver dollar.

Enlisted men stationed at Fort Griffin and one former soldier also were killed. One death in a saloon on Main

[6] "Frontier Life of John Chadbourne Irwin," as cited.

147

Street grew out of a poker game between a Fort Griffin lieutenant and a soldier. The soldier won and started out of the saloon. He was shot in the back and the lieutenant was later absolved of guilt. Another killing resulted from a drunken row between a captain and an enlisted man. The captain killed the soldier and was presently acquitted because "it was the only dignified thing he could do under the circumstances."

The third instance occurred when a former soldier called "Scotty" and a local outlaw quarreled. Later, the outlaw obtained a gun and went to Scotty's home. When the latter saw the armed man coming, he fled around his house with the gunman in pursuit. Scotty's wife was working over a wash tub, and when the outlaw came in hot pursuit, Scotty ran directly to her. Falling on her knees, she begged the outlaw not to kill her husband. But her pleadings fell on deaf ears; the gunman deliberately killed him before her eyes.

While District Court was in session at Fort Griffin, even a woman's name was added to the lengthening list of murderers. She killed a drunken Lipan Indian for stumbling into her rooming house. It was only upon her earnest request that she was tried. She, too, was acquitted.[7]

The names of trail-driving cowboys were also inscrolled on the Flat's death roll. John Chadbourne Irwin later said that during the buffalo and trail herd days, the civil authorities were either helpless to remedy conditions or were controlled by the lawless element. During those days killings were frequent, and Irwin himself helped bury a number of cowboys killed in shooting scrapes.[8]

[7] This summary of killings is found in Biggers, *Shackelford County Sketches*. The list is found in the "Old Fort Griffin" part of the book.

The cowboys must have seen Griffin as did Bill Akers, who drove into town in January, 1877, and stopped at Uncle Charlie Sebastian's Bison Hotel.[9] He had developed a healthy appetite from his long ride, and he enjoyed a hotel supper of baked, fried, and roasted buffalo, and venison and other good things. Early next morning he was up to see the town; but he saw nothing "very attractively beautiful to gaze upon," nothing except "a few dobie and picket houses, corrals, and immense stacks of buffalo hides."[10]

At that time the post on the hill, a quarter of a mile south, was almost depopulated, there being but one company of Negro soldiers stationed there. The days of scout patrols, of escort duty with surveying parties and wagon trains, and of campaigning against hostile Indians were gone, and the Negro troopers now had little to do but drill, occasionally stand inspection, quarrel and fight with the Flat's toughs, and twiddle their thumbs.

But the Flat was coming into its own. Business structures were springing up along Main Street like overnight mushrooms. F. E. Conrad's store rooms comprised the most extensive establishment. There the buffalo hunters bought their supplies and sold their flint hides. "Imagine," wrote Akers," a huge rambling house of rooms, crowded with merchandise; with fourth or fifth wagons waiting to be loaded, and perhaps a hundred hunters purchasing supplies. We are told that yesterday's sales amounted to nearly $4,000, about $2,500 of which was spent for guns and ammunition."

Conrad was a merchant prince, widely known as a

[8] "Frontier Life of John Chadbourne Irwin," as cited.

[9] *Ibid.* The word *uncle* was commonly applied to elderly men of good standing in the community.

[10] *Fort Worth Democrat,* January 25, 1877.

frontier post trader and merchant, catering to soldiers, buffalo hunters, farmers, ranchers, and trail drivers. He was born at Rockford, Illinois, in 1842, and spent much of his childhood in Tampa, Florida, where at the outbreak of the Civil War he was a clerk in his uncle's store. He served during the war with Hood's Texas Brigade. After the conflict, he was appointed post trader at Fort McKavett and remained there until 1870; then he came to Fort Griffin, to be associated with Charley Rath in the sutler store. At this post he did a thriving business with Mackenzie's troopers during the period 1872–75, then with the buffalo hunters. He grubstaked the hunters who came to him for guns, ammunition, and provisions, advanced them cash, and accepted their orders for cash payments to their employees. And since he was the town's banker, he purchased a large safe in which all his patrons could keep their money.[11]

When the trail herds first arrived in Griffin, Conrad and Rath's store was the community's main provisioning establishment, and later, after the store was moved to the Flat, Charley Rath sold his interest to Conrad and went to Kansas.[12] But the store continued to enjoy its favor with the cowmen.

No doubt, the Flat's most deadly shooting spree, in which two cowboys, Billy Bland and Charley Reed from the Millett ranch, were involved, occurred on January 17, 1877. A traveling salesman, Howard W. Peak, had just ar-

[11] Reynolds to Webb, January 27, 1947.

[12] The *Fort Griffin Echo*, February 21, 1880, carried an announcement that "Mr. Charles Rath, one of the oldest and most respected citizens, late of the firm of Conrad & Rath, left here Wednesday night for his new home in Dodge City, Kansas." Early in 1879 the partners had moved their $40,000 stock of merchandise to the Flat. See also Albany, Texas, *Minutes of the Commissioners Court,* Vol. I (August 12, 1879), 234.

rived at Griffin to sell his wares to local merchants. Frank Conrad and other townsmen had told him about the Bee Hive Saloon, which he described as a "double one-storied," adobe combination "saloon, gambling house, and dance hall." Attracted by curiosity, he visited it. He had just arrived when the two cowboys got into a scrap with local authorities "and commenced 'to draw,' whereupon I beat a hasty retreat to the hotel."[13]

Presently he learned what had happened. The *Frontier Echo* of January 19, 1877, played down the Bee Hive affair under a small-type heading, "Shooting Bee at Fort Griffin," stating that "one man, a stranger in the place, was killed instantly and Billy Bland, a cowboy; Lieutenant Myers, late of the 10th Cavalry, and a Mr. Jeffries, County Attorney of Shackelford, were wounded."

The *Dallas Daily Herald* carried a more realistic and extended account, which was written by a Griffin correspondent, whose pen name was "Comanche Jim." Griffin citizens, he said, had witnessed a tragedy at Donnelly and Carroll's varieties. Bland and Reed, "full of old rye and the devil," had attempted "to run the town." They had ridden recklessly into town and had fired their Colts several times to impress the citizenry. Then they entered the Bee Hive, drank heavily, and began to flourish their six-shooters. The proprietors protested and urged them not to start trouble. "Their racket was suddenly stopped," said Comanche Jim, "by the appearance of Deputy Sheriff Crozier [W. R. Cruger], and County Attorney [William] Jeffries, who, as officers of the law, commanded them to put up their guns or leave."

[13] Howard W. Peak, "On the Road Fifty Years Ago," *Bunker's Monthly*, Vol. II (August, 1928), 15.

Then, he continued, "the order seemed to be the signal for the ball then closed to open in a different way. About ten shots were fired in rapid succession, with unfortunately more injury to innocent spectators than to the guilty parties." A former lieutenant of the Tenth Cavalry named Myers was shot through the back and died about two hours afterwards. A young lawyer, Dan Barron, who had lately been married, was shot in the center of the forehead and died instantly. Jeffries was shot about three inches above the heart, but did not die. Cruger received a slight wound.

Comanche Jim finished his story by saying: "Reed, after emptying his pistol, one shot of which, as was proved by his position, must have killed the young man Barron, got away and is still at liberty. . . . Though too late to witness the shooting, a fact by no means to be regretted, I was in time to see Mr. Jeffries led away; Barron on the ground, with his brains oozing through the hole in his forehead; Lieutenant Myers dying, reclining on his side, and Bland rolling on his back in agony. All from the effects of a drunken spree and the useless habit of packing a six-shooter. . . . The excuse that Fort Griffin is a frontier town and that Indians are dangerous is now getting 'too thin' to justify men necessarily carrying weapons, which, as a matter of consequence, they use when frontier whiskey makes them feel like it."[14]

After the shooting, Reed ran out the front door and on to Clampett's wagon yard where he had tied his horse. But by this time angry men were swarming out of the saloon to find him. He did not attempt to reach his horse; instead,

---

[14] *Dallas Daily Herald*, January 25, 1887; Herron's "Recollections and Experiences of Frontier Life," as cited; "Newt B. Jones," in J. R. Webb Papers (MS, R. N. Richardson Collection, Hardin-Simmons University).

he vaulted over the back fence and fled westward on foot. Next day he showed up at Newt B. Jones's line camp near the Mackenzie Crossing of the Clear Fork, twelve miles from the Flat, where he gave his account of the shooting. He said that Bland started the shooting just for fun, but when Cruger sought to arrest him the fight began.

Reed was given a gun and horse at the line camp, and hid out for the rest of the day. The following morning he was on the move again, after Jones had cooked him some "chuck," and furnished him a pack horse. Then he left the country.[15]

This Bee Hive shooting spree was characteristic of the lawlessness along the entire Texas frontier, in part an aftermath of the Civil War. As early as December 23, 1872, the Texas Adjutant General, F. L. Britton, had warned Governor Edmond J. Davis that in one month 238 felonies had been committed in only sixty-eight counties. "Small boys," he said, "wore six-shooters to school, and no one considered himself safe in the absence of a young arsenal strapped about his person."[16] Henry Herron, once peace officer at the Flat, declared that nearly all men and some women carried Colt revolvers during his stay there.

Outlaws were numerous. If they were too closely pressed by officers of the law, they "found a secure and convenient harbor of refuge by simply crossing the Río Grande or passing into the Indian Territory, where their recapture was almost impossible."[17]

Griffin had drawn more than its share of border riff-

[15] *Ibid.*

[16] *Report* of the Adjutant General for the State of Texas for the Year 1872 (Austin, 1872), 9; J. R. Webb Papers (MS, R. N. Richardson Collection, Hardin-Simmons University).

[17] *Ibid.*

raff, for Shackelford County peace officers and courts could not curb them. As early as April, 1876, Comanche Jim noticed the rise of a vigilance committee. He said that it was impossible for local citizens "to keep their horses by locking," so they had "at last resorted to the expedient of not only locking but tying up those caught stealing them."[18] The *Dallas Daily Herald* of April 23, 1876, reported that a vigilance committee at the Flat was astonishing the authorities, both military and civil, by the offhand way it did business.

The *Fort Worth Democrat* of April 22, 1876, also carried Griffin news under the signature of "Lone Star" and a date line of April 11. Lone Star stated that, on April 2, Bill Henderson's gang of horse thieves had stolen twenty-six head of horses from Ellison, Dewees, and Bishop's cattle herd near the Mackenzie crossing of the Clear Fork, and that a party of "Low Boys" and Tonkaway Indians had organized and gone in pursuit. The thieves were accompanied by a Griffin prostitute called Sally Watson. A part of the thieving band was overhauled on Croton Creek in western Haskell County, eighty miles away, and Joe Watson, "Red," "Larapie Dan," and a man named Burr were taken in tow.

Henderson had previously divided his crowd; with one group he had continued on the move with the major part of the stolen stock, "leaving the other portion to follow more leisurely with the sweet scented female and a wagon and team which they had in their possession."

Lone Star stated that the "Low Boys" returned to Griffin, "reaching this place yesterday with one prisoner (Burr) —the other three having 'got away' as the boys expressed

[18] *Dallas Daily Herald,* April 29, 1876.

it." Burr claimed to be a buffalo hunter, and as the "boys" could not prove that he belonged to the thieving gang, they allowed him to get away. Henderson, "Kansas Bill," and Hank Floyd and another thief escaped. Later Henderson and Floyd were traced to Dodge City, arrested, and returned to Albany, then the seat of Shackelford County. On Friday night, June 3, about fifty vigilantes took them from the jail, after they had overpowered the sheriff and jailor, and hanged them from an elm-tree limb on Hubbard Creek, a short distance from town.[19]

In April, the vigilantes posted written notices "intimating that the presence of 'Long Kate,' 'Big Billy,' Ellen Gentry, Minnie Gray, and Sally Watson, prostitutes, and 'Pony' Spencer and Tom Riley, general 'rustlers,'" was obnoxious to Griffin citizens, and warned them to leave by a given hour. A hideous caricature of a death's head and crossbones in sanguinary colors embellished the poster—suggestive of summary action by the vigilantes if they did not comply with their orders. The notices accelerated their departure.[20]

This same Griffin newsgatherer also reported that the vigilantes had hanged Houston Foughts and Charley McBride for horse stealing. Comanche Jim said that McBride was "caught in the very act of taking what wasn't 'his'n.'" He said that "a pick and shovel may be seen underneath the rotting body, a silent hint, I presume, to the sympathetic spectator to cut down, if he wishes, and inter the blackened

[19] *Denison Daily News,* June 4, 1876; *Frontier Echo,* June 9, 1876; Herron's "Recollections and Experiences of Frontier Life," as cited.

[20] *Fort Worth Democrat,* April 29, 1876. It is possible that "Long Kate" was none other than Kate Gamble or "Indian Kate," who stood in with certain officers of the law for protection, and whose shanty was a rendezvous for cutthroats and murderers. See Herron's "Recollections and Experiences of Frontier Life," as cited.

and hideous corpse.[21] . . . A party of horse thieves, headed by a young man named Watson, having stolen a considerable bunch of horses from a cattle outfit, were pursued and overtaken by a party of citizens and soldiers. The fate of the thieves is a mystery. The prevalent idea is, they have gone to a land where horses will not be required, *quien sabe."*

Comanche Jim admitted, however, that the vigilance committee had done one good thing: it had broken up a nest of prostitutes, and the soiled birds had flown. The vigilantes had been motivated by the idea that bad meat draws flies, in the persons of horse thieves and desperadoes.

Two other reports indicate that they kept up their disagreeable "house cleaning." In early May, 1876, a notorious horse thief known as "Reddy" was captured in Indian Territory and brought back to Fort Griffin and put in the guardhouse until he could be surrendered to Eastland County authorities, for he had stolen a horse in that county. Here he was turned over to an armed party to finish his journey; the next day his body was found hanging to a tree three miles from the post.[22]

The *Fort Worth Democrat* of December 19, 1876, indicated that horse stealing in the Fort Griffin country was still hazardous. It reported that the vigilantes had just captured and hanged, about seven miles west of Griffin, eleven horse thieves whom they had been trailing for some time.

[21] *Dallas Daily Herald*, April 29, 1876. A. B. Greenleaf, visiting in the Fort Griffin country at this time, saw McBride's body hanging to the limb of a pecan tree. To it was pinned a piece of paper on which was written: "He said his name was McBride, but he was a liar as well as a thief." See *Ten Years in Texas* (Selma, Alabama, 1880), 35.

[22] *Frontier Echo*, May 12, 1876.

They were overtaken with twenty-seven head of horses. No mercy was shown them. Four others, belonging to the same gang, were overtaken beyond Red River, just south of Fort Sill. The *Democrat* stated that they were being returned to Griffin, and expressed doubt that they would long enjoy good health.

Within a year the settlers of the Fort Griffin country found themselves aligned, actually or in sympathy, with one or the other of two hostile groups. The vigilance committee was supported by those seeking to stamp out lawlessness and the rival group by thieves, gamblers, prostitutes, and ne'er-do-wells. There could be no middle ground. If one sought to be neutral he was regarded with suspicion by both warring factions.

Open warfare brought Texas Rangers hurrying to Griffin. Captain G. W. Campbell headed the twenty-five or thirty Rangers as in a column of twos they rode down Griffin's dusty street. But on this first visit they did not tarry long. They established a camp on Elm Creek, near the site of Throckmorton; they then moved to Camp Sibley, on a creek by that name, near its junction with the Clear Fork and about ten miles northeast of Fort Griffin. In the spring of 1878, the camp was moved again, this time near Oglesby Peak on the north side of the Clear Fork and about three or four miles from Griffin. In July, 1878, Lieutenant G. W. Arrington arrived to supersede Campbell in command. Major John B. Jones ordered him to guard his men against any undue sympathy or prejudice against the parties to the feud in that section.[23] Without question, the Rangers

[23] Major Jones to Lieutenant G. W. Arrington, July 13, 1878 (MS in files of the Adjutant General, Austin, Texas).

brought a moderating influence to the Flat; they were fair and objective in their work and partial only in maintaining law and order.

One person who suffered from the activity of the vigilance committee was John Larn. Larn had come to Griffin in the early 1870's as a lad sixteen years of age. He had a pleasing personality, good nerve, and was a splendid marksman. A few years later he wooed and married a prominent rancher's daughter, and, by 1874, he had accumulated a fine herd of cattle, had located on the Clear Fork, and had received a contract to supply Fort Griffin with beef. His cattle-raising career lasted only a short four years, however. In 1878, he was accused by surrounding farmers of being a cattle thief and even a murderer. He was eventually arrested and taken to Albany, the county seat, but before ever being tried in court, he was shot to death by a mob of twenty men who broke into the building where he was imprisoned.[24] His innocence or guilt was never proved. He was a victim of the impetuous and high-handed frontier "justice" that the vigilance committee dispensed.

Yet vigilantes and outlaws did not stop the cattle's cloven hooves from pounding the Western Trail by Fort Griffin. The hard-visaged trail drivers had been trained in a school of hard knocks, of lonely and dangerous toil, and had met and dealt with both good and bad men. To find relief from lonely trail driving, they sought Griffin's motley, milling crowds, drank fiery whiskey in the saloons, and found color and life about the gaming tables. Night life

[24] *Galveston News,* July 13, 1878; "Early History Notes," in J. R. Webb Papers (MS, R. N. Richardson Collection, Hardin-Simmons University); *Fort Worth Democrat,* June 26 and July 2, 1878; *Frontier Echo,* July 5, 1878.

here was all that they had expected. They met, fought, and gambled with dissolute men, and came to know, and be taken in by, the denizens of the town—barkeepers, game dealers, and pitiful creatures who had once been women. When once the huge kerosene ceiling lamps were lighted, fiddles were tuned, and toughened frontiersmen and tougher, hard-faced, calico-gowned, straight-haired women moved onto the dance floor or found their places about the gaming tables, or in the saloon, the cowmen joined them for either dangerous games or frolic.[25]

How many cattle went up the Western Trail from 1875 to 1880 no one knows. About 450,000 head of Captain John F. Lytle's cattle poured over the trail past Fort Griffin, and Colonel Ike T. Pryor drove northward 30,000 more. And still others—George W. Saunders, later president of the Texas Trail Drivers Association, Shanghai Pierce, Seth Mabry, Doc Burnet, Dan Waggoner, John and Ab Blocker —also sent or drove herds northward. Saunders later stated that of the twelve million cattle and horses that went to the northern markets during the trail-driving days, six million crossed Red River at Doan's Crossing, on the Western Trail; five million at Red River Station, on the Chisholm Trail; and one million at other points on that river. The sale of these vast herds brought $250,000,000 back to Texas,[26] al-

[25] V. O. Key, "A Journalist of the Texas Frontier," *Bunker's Monthly*, Vol. II, No. 2, (September, 1928).

[26] Paul I. Wellman, *The Trampling Herd* (New York, 1939), 225; E. E. Dale, *The Range Cattle Industry* (Norman, 1930), 59ff., 64. Professor Dale states that "perhaps the best known and longest [trail] used . . . was the old western trail to Dodge City and Ogalalla, Nebraska." It ran past Fort Griffin, crossed Red River near Doan's Store, on through Old Greer County, a corner of the Comanche-Kiowa reservation, the Cheyenne-Arapaho reservation and through the Cherokee Outlet to Dodge City, or even farther, to Ogalalla.

though a fraction of that amount must have been expended for cowboy wages and for supplies at Griffin and elsewhere.

Such a heavy movement brought Griffin an ever increasing trade and wealth during the driving season of each year. This was supplemented by a year-round trade in buffalo hides and meat, with Griffin being used largely as a clearing center.

By 1878, Griffin, or the Flat, became a boom town largely because it had the advantages of these two sources of wealth. "Captain" G. W. Robson, described as a "dried-up, 'fiesty' " little man, saw that Griffin was blossoming into a bustling town and moved his newspaper from Jacksboro to Griffin. He proclaimed in the first issue of the *Fort Griffin Echo* on January 4, 1879, that he would "work for the prosperity of Shackelford County and its inhabitants, . . . and especially for the Live Stock interests." To do this, by small type face he played down outlawry and crime, and joined in friendly, and sometimes angry, banter and debate with rival West Texas editors, particularly with the celebrated Edgar Rye of the *Albany News*. Robson believed that the cowboy was a vidette "on the extreme outpost of Civilization" and that Griffin had become his headquarters. Believing this, he helped to make Griffin the leading cowtown.[27] He had previously helped to stage an annual session of the North Texas Cattle Raisers' Association at Griffin in 1878.

[27] W. C. Holden, "Frontier Journalism in West Texas," *Southwestern Historical Quarterly,* Vol. XXXII (January, 1929), 206ff.; *Frontier Echo,* December 1, 1878; Robson had published the *Echo* for three years at Jacksboro, Texas, stayed three years at Griffin, after which he published at Albany, Texas, until the *Echo* was consolidated with the *Albany Star.*

IX Griffin, Hide Town Entrepôt

B Y 1880, ORDERLY LIFE was rapidly supplanting outlawry and crime in the Flat. The days of pistol-popping
just to impress the Griffinites were practically over. An
amusing incident proved that this was true. Two cowboys,
who said that they were canine offspring from Jones County, wild and woolly, thought that they would run the town
and get up a first-class shooting scrape. But Johnny Ham-
mond, acting constable during the absence of Constable
Cal Walker, landed them in the "cooler." Next morning
Judge Steele held a matinee for their special benefit, for
which they contributed $15.50 each. Editor G. W. Robson
was amused. "Come to town as often as you want to, boys,"
he invited them. "But do not try to run it. You will be
left every time."[1]

Business was temporarily dull. As early as March, 1878,
Griffin merchants had complained of dull times because no
buffalo hides were being brought to town. The hunters
assured them, however, that the buffalo would again seek
the Staked Plains and the rangeland below the Caprock

[1] *Fort Griffin Echo*, February 14, 1880.

when spring grass was good. Then Griffin "could have lively times with the hunters and cowboys."

If at that time Robson saw destiny's handwriting on the wall for Jacksboro, he continued to whistle merrily through his walrus mustache, but soon came his move from Jacksboro to Griffin, an up-and-coming town. In August, he attended the Northwest Texas Cattlemen's Association at Griffin and was entertained in fine style in Jack Schwartz's Planters House, although he also had kind words for that town's new Occidental Hotel, for it carried a substantial advertisement in the *Echo*.[2]

Robson was not aware of the fact that Griffin's current boom was even more temporary than Jacksboro's had been. Soldiers at the near-by fort would soon haul down their flag and march away for the last time, the buffalo-hide industry had already reached its peak, and the cattle drives over the Western Trail via Griffin would shortly diminish. Then Griffin would have little chance for successful competition with the flourishing county seat of Albany, eighteen miles farther south.

It was not foresight and planning on the part of Griffin businessmen that had made their town the major supply center for the trail drivers between San Antonio and Dodge City, nor had they made possible the profitable buffalo-hide and meat industries; both had been fortuitous, unexpected —and temporary—blessings.

Yet Griffin hunters little thought that the many thousands of buffalo would soon be destroyed. For decades past, the buffalo had ranged undiminished on the frontier. William T. Hornaday, onetime superintendent of the National Zoological Park, has well said that "of all the quadrupeds

[2] *Ibid.*, March 15, 1878.

that have lived upon the earth, probably no other species has ever marshalled such innumerable hosts as those of the American bison."[3] It would have been just as easy to count the leaves on the trees of a forest as the Great Plains bison at any given time prior to 1870.

By 1850, the buffalo were divided into the Northern and Southern herds,[4] each containing several million animals. The range of the Southern herd extended, north to south, from the Platte River to the Río Grande, and, east to west, from about the ninety-eighth meridian to the Rocky Mountains. Each herd moved slowly northward in the spring and southward in the fall, leisurely feeding on buffalo, grama, mesquite, and bluestem grasses, but preferably on buffalograss, because of its nutritious quality, which was not impaired by the withering heat of summer or the snows of winter.

The vast grassland south of Red River during the 1870's was the principal range of the Southern herd, for in much of this area winter favored the bison. Snow seldom covered the range, and occasionally when it did, it soon melted, thereby uncovering the grass-carpeted ground for the always hungry buffalo.

[3] William T. Hornaday, *The Extermination of the American Bison* (Washington, 1889), 387.

[4] Captain Howard Stansbury had noticed the division of the great herd in 1851, which he implied had been caused by the constant stream of Argonauts and Mormons passing over the Platte trails. See "Exploration and Survey of the Valley of the Great Salt Lake of Utah," 32 Cong., Special sess., *Sen. Ex. Doc. 3*, 246. Actually, these two divisions were not herds, except while on their spring and fall migrations; each was composed of small herds of from fifty to two hundred or more while grazing. J. A. Allen, "History of the American Bison," in the *Ninth Annual Report of the United States Geological and Geographical Survey of the Territories, Embracing Colorado and Parts of Adjacent Territories; Being a Report of Progress of the Exploration for the Year 1875* (3 parts, Washington, 1877), III, 530ff.

So long as the nomadic Indians had roamed about over the Great Plains, the buffalo had been their commissary. It supplied them with food; they drank its blood; they made glue, cups, spoons, and trinkets from buffalo horns; they used buffalo hides for tipi coverings, robes, beds, bow-strings, lariats, sacks, and travois beds; they wove buffalo hair into reatas, belts, and personal ornaments. Even the dried droppings of the bison, or "buffalo chips," were indispensable for fuel, for most of the Great Plains was treeless.[5]

For decades prior to the Civil War, both Indian and white hunters had used buffalo robes as media of exchange. In 1845, Captain John C. Frémont published statistics furnished him by a member of the American Fur Company showing that during the preceding decade the Indians had sold (bartered) annually 90,000 bison hides from the Upper Missouri region alone. Since these hides were best for robes only for four months of each year, it was estimated that the Indians had slaughtered during the full year about 120,000 buffalo in that region, or 1,200,000 in the preceding decade. Throughout the Great Plains they must have killed annually at least 500,000 bison,[6] or 5,000,000 for this ten year period.

Just when white hunters made serious inroads on the Southern herd would be hard to say. In 1835, Josiah Gregg mentioned that they were slaughtering buffalo recklessly; nineteen years later W. B. Parker, who had accompanied Randolph B. Marcy on his reconnaissance of western Texas to locate sites for Indian reservations, stated that "this animal [the bison] is rapidly disappearing from the plains."[7]

[5] Frederick W. Hodge, ed., *Handbook of the American Indians North of Mexico* (2 vols., Washington, 1907), I, 170.
[6] Allen, "History of the American Bison," in the *Ninth Annual Report*

But the slaughter of the bison by both Indian and white hunters prior to the Civil War was small compared with that of the 1870's. Hornaday believed that as the herds existed in 1870, 500,000 head of young and old bulls could have been killed every year for twenty years without appreciably reducing the size of the herds.[8] But within this decade hide hunters wiped out the Southern herd of about 5,000,000 animals. Indeed, their wanton destruction of the Southern herd was one reason for Comanche and Kiowa hostility during the early 1870's. Hunters moving southward from Dodge City, and others from Griffin and elsewhere along the Texas frontier moving westward, were cutting deeply into two sides of the Southern herd.

J. Wright Mooar, whose hide-hunting was both in Kansas and in western Texas, has left an arresting account of the rise and decline of this industry. Mooar was born in Vermont of Scotch parents, and at the age of nineteen sought adventure and fortune in the West. He arrived at Fort Hays, Kansas, a federal outpost on Big Creek (a tributary of Smoky River), in the fall of 1870, where he found employment as a government woodcutter on Walnut Creek, about thirty miles south of the fort. This job was too hum-

of the United States Geological and Geographical Survey, III, 561–62; "Agriculture," *United States Patent Office Report* (1851–52), II, 125.

[7] Josiah Gregg, *Commerce of the Prairies* (2 vols., New York, 1844), II, 125; W. B. Parker, *Notes Taken during the Expedition Commanded by R. B. Marcy, U. S. A.* (Philadelphia, 1856), 101–102.

[8] Hornaday, *The Extermination of the American Bison*, 435. Another thought that the projection of the Union Pacific, the Kansas Pacific, and the Atchison, Topeka, and Santa Fe railroads into the very heart of the buffalo country hastened the destruction of both herds, for these roads made possible the transportation and marketing of the hides. See Richard Irving Dodge, *Our Wild Indians* (Hartford, 1883), 293.

drum and he presently changed to buffalo hunting to supply Fort Hays with meat.[9]

At this time Charley Rath and A. C. Myers were Indian traders, swapping trade goods for buffalo hides, which
they sold at a good profit to W. C. Lobenstein of Leavenworth, Kansas. Shortly Lobenstein informed the two traders
that an English firm had asked him to send them 500 "flint"
buffalo hides for a leather-making experiment. If it was
successful, the firm would ask him to deliver many thousand more hides.

Lobenstein called upon Rath and Myers to supply him
with the necessary number of hides, which they bought
from J. Wright Mooar and other hunters in the field. After
Mooar had helped to fill this order, he still had left fifty-
seven hides. Then he wondered if his brother John and
brother-in-law, John W. Combs, who lived in New York
City, might not dispose of them. Soon he wrote to them,
stating that he was shipping to New York his left-over hides
and asking that they try to sell them to a New England
tanner. When the hides arrived, John and Combs sold them
to two Pennsylvania tanners for $3.50 per hide. The tanners
promised that if they could convert the hides into leather,
they would give them an order for many others. The experiment was successful and the Mooar brothers were
asked to supply two thousand additional buffalo hides.[10]

Both the American and the English experiments were

[9] J. Wright Mooar, "Buffalo Days," *Holland's Magazine* (January,
1933), 13. Mooar told his story to James Winford Hunt, who, in turn,
edited it.

[10] Lydia Louise Mooar, "Mooar Family," in Mooar Papers (MS,
Texas Technological College Museum), 3. Fortunately, both J. Wright
and John Mooar's experiences have been recorded, and will be cited on
later pages of this narrative.

successful, and the way was paved for the slaughter of the Great Plains buffalo, for the hide-hunters had difficulty supplying the growing demand. So lucrative was this new industry that presently hundreds of hunters, armed with powerful guns, were swarming out from Dodge City and Griffin in large and small parties, to join in the great hunt.[11] They came by wagon, on horseback, and afoot, singly and in bands of four, five, or more to begin their work of slaughter.[12]

John Mooar resigned his New York clerkship and hurried to Kansas to join his brother, J. Wright Mooar, and Charley Wright in a buffalo-hunting partnership. J. Wright Mooar advanced $250 to each partner to enter the new firm on an equal footing with him. He was to kill the game, and they were to do the freighting, marketing, and looking after the camp. When the partnership was formed, they hired three men to serve as skinners, bought a wagon and supplies, and headed for Kiowa Creek to begin their operations.

The Mooar brothers realized the need for a long-range gun, more powerful than any rifle on the market. John wrote to Sharp's Rifle Company of Bridgeport, Connecticut, about the matter, explaining the kind of gun necessary for buffalo hunting. After this company had tried out two or three experimental rifles and had found them unsatisfactory, it developed the much-needed rifle, which weighed from twelve to sixteen pounds. It was of .50–1.10 caliber, and accommodated a long brass shell containing 110 grains of powder, which hurled its leaden missiles to incredible

[11] The Mooar brothers carried in the field well-equipped parties, with large Murphy wagons filled with supplies to last for several weeks of hunting. Each Murphy wagon could trail smaller hunters' wagons. See J. Wright Mooar, "Buffalo Days," *Holland's Magazine* (January, 1933), 22.

[12] Dodge, *Our Wild Indians*, 293.

distances. Mooar's gun cost $150, but later, when manu-
factured in quantity, it sold for $50. The Springfield, Spen-
cer, Henry, and other rifles were also used for buffalo
hunting.[13]

Many other hide-procuring outfits were organized and
moved west, southwest, and south of Fort Dodge to make
contact with the Southern herd. For a short time the Mooar-
Wright outfit met with little success, for the buffalo had
drifted into the Texas Panhandle, and Wright abandoned
the partnership for a more lucrative trading venture.

All the Kansas hunters were discouraged. Where was
the Southern herd? Some thought that it was extinct, and
others argued that it had drifted southward. J. Wright
Mooar decided to find out. He asked John Webb to go
with him into *Comanchería,* where these migrant animals
might be found. Webb accepted the invitation, and the
two men saddled their favorite mounts and rode southward,
carrying no supplies except a sack of salt and plenty of
ammunition. Their food would be "buffalo straight."

They crossed the Kansas boundary line and into old
"No Man's Land," now the Panhandle of Oklahoma. But
they did not stop there. They were in search of the Southern
herd. They forded the Beaver, at a point twenty miles east
of where the little village of that name was soon to be built,
then Wolf Creek, a prong of the North Canadian, where,
"in this lonely land," Mooar later said, "we found the great
herd, millions upon millions, fattening on the grass of those
mighty uplands." For five days the two men rode through
and camped in "a mobile sea of living buffalo."

[13] See *Holland's Magazine* (May, 1933), 12. Hunters also carried a
stick or tripod upon which to rest the heavy guns, particularly when they
became hot from constant firing.

Then they returned to Dodge City to carry the exciting news of their discovery. After the buffalo hunters had counseled together, they decided to send a delegation to call on the commanding officer at the fort. Mooar stated later that he received them courteously and inquired about their hunting experiences. Finally, said Mooar, he asked the all-important question: "Major, if we cross into Texas, what will be the government's attitude toward us?" "Boys," he replied, "if I were a buffalo hunter, I would hunt buffalo where buffalo are!"

The hunters did not stand on ceremony; they hurried away to make preparations for the great hunt. The Mooars were among those moving southward, with four teams and ten men. They set out for the Texas plains, and pitched camp for a time on a small stream in Hansford County, and then moved farther southward, "striking four miles west of the old ruins of the John C. Frémont and Kit Carson Adobe Walls."[14]

In March, 1874, Charley Myers left Dodge City with a wagon train of trade goods pulled by eight six-yoke ox-teams to establish a supply base at the old adobe ruins in Hutchinson County, Texas, on the north bank of the South Canadian, about sixteen miles southeast of the present town of Stinnett. About forty hunters and teamsters erected there a stockade corral, in one corner of which they built a cottonwood-log storehouse. In April, Charley Rath also built near by a sod house for a branch store, south of Myers'. Jim Hanrahan then came with a stock of whiskey for a

[14] Five years earlier Mooar had correctly stated that "these were supposed to have been the remains of a former trading post with the Indians built by the traders of Bent's Fort on the Arkansas River." See "Frontier Experiences of J. Wright Mooar," *West Texas Historical Association Year Book*, Vol. IV (June, 1928), 89.

saloon in between these two competitors, and Tom O'Keefe erected a picket blacksmith shop.[15] This settlement was the "Adobe Walls" which the Quahada Comanches and their allies attacked a few weeks later, an account of which is found in a preceding chapter.

The Mooar brothers disposed of their "flint" hides and meat at Dodge City, but they also established a hunting camp at Adobe Walls. From here, J. Wright Mooar with five other hunters moved eastward to Gagesby Creek, a tributary of the Washita, and established a base within the buffalo country, where they were attacked by the Comanches. But the warriors found the hunters' long-range buffalo guns too much for them and gave up the fight. Then Mooar's party moved southward to the North Fork of the Red River. Here they killed 666 bison, which John and "Dirty Face" Jones loaded and trailed back to Adobe Walls. While there, they learned for the first time of Quanah Parker's attack. They made other kills on the Cimarron, but they realized that the main herd had moved again. They searched for it along Beaver Creek in No Man's Land, then in the Texas Panhandle where they had a successful hunt, and finally they dropped back to Beaver Creek for a winter camp. During several months of hunting, they had met with considerable success, and the next spring their heavily laden bull wagons pulled out for Dodge City loaded with flint hides.

Then J. Wright Mooar decided that, since the buffalo had moved southward, he would leave the southwestern Kansas–Texas Panhandle area. He would get on the southern flank of the great herd, at a place in western Texas un-

[15] See sketch of buildings drawn by John W. Mooar, in 1917, in Mooar Papers (MS, Texas Technological College Museum).

known to most of the Kansas hide hunters. Therefore, after
he had sold his choice cuts of meat at Wichita and El Do-
rado, Kansas, he continued southward across Indian Territory to Denison, Texas, where he traded some of his
mules for oxen and bought additional wagons.

From here he shoved off on his new venture with
twelve heavily loaded wagons, six laden with his own supplies and six with Fort Griffin freight. Along the road,
running southwestward via Decatur and Jacksboro, he was
impressed by the grim, silent monuments of Indian atroc-
ity—smut-blackened chimneys of what once had been
frontiersmen's homes, and beyond Jacksboro, the burned
wagons of Warren's train. But he and his teamsters met no
Indians. They arrived at Fort Griffin without mishap, delivered their government freight, and made preparations to
leave on a buffalo hunt.

When Colonel George Buell, commander at Fort Griffin, learned of Mooar's plans, he warned him not to travel
far within the buffalo country. Mooar replied that he would
assume all responsibility for his actions. He later wrote
that he and Buell had "quite a tilt of words." Buell ordered
him not to go more than twenty miles from the post,[16] but
Mooar ignored his order.

Mooar moved up the Clear Fork, accompanied by
John, and four employees, White and Russell, Mike
O'Brien, and John Goff. They crossed Paint Creek into
present Haskell County, and established a hunting camp
near what is now the village of Weinert, where they met
with great success in hunting. In November, 1874, John
returned to Denison with his Murphy wagons loaded with

[16] "Frontier Experiences of J. Wright Mooar," *West Texas Historical
Association Year Book*, Vol. IV (June, 1928), 90.

flint hides. Three wagons, each pulled by six oxen, were required to haul this enormous hide accumulation. In Denison, however, John found no hide market, and the banks would not advance him money on the hides. He therefore wired Lobenstein of Leavenworth, who bought the hides and sent him the necessary remittance.

When Kansas hunters learned of Mooar's success in western Texas, they came hurrying southward. "That fall," Mooar stated, "other hunters came from Dodge and about a dozen outfits of different sizes went out from Fort Griffin to hunt buffalo."[17]

By 1876, dealers in hides and hunters' supplies also moved into western Texas. Charley Rath's wagon train with supplies, lumber, nails, and tools crossed the Double Mountain Fork of the Brazos south of the mountains by that name. John Russell's train of fifty wagons, each drawn by six yoke of oxen and loaded with all kinds of hunters' supplies, followed Rath's. About eighty hunters, whom Rath had supplied in Kansas, also came, including such successful hunters as Hank Campbell, Mortimer ("Wild Bill") Kress, John Smith, Joe Freed, Willis Crawford, Harry Burns, and Sol Rees.

J. Wright Mooar has explained that in the fall of 1876 Charley Rath and Robert M. Wright, the Fort Dodge sutler, formed a partnership with the Lee and Reynolds firm to exploit the western Texas buffalo-hide industry, and that they transferred a part of their stock from Dodge City to Mobeetie, in the Texas Panhandle, where they were joined by fifty or sixty hunters with wagons. And from here, when the buffalo moved southward, they followed them to the

[17] *Ibid.*, 91; J. Wright Mooar, "Buffalo Days," *Holland's Magazine* (January, 1933), 22.

Double Mountain country in Stonewall County. Saloon operators, dance-hall outfits with about forty women, and ne'er-do-wells also came. They located their hide-buying and hunter-supplying center south of the Double Mountain Fork of the Brazos, about fourteen miles southwest of what is now Hamlin, Texas, and on what was later the Pringle Moore ranch.[18]

Shortly Camp Reynolds, or Rath City, as some of the hunters called it, consisted of six sod huts spaced irregularly on both sides of the Fort Griffin road. On the north side of the road and about one hundred yards from the nearest sod house was a sod corral, in one corner of which was a small bunkhouse or guardhouse. The two buildings on the same side of the road, from west to east, were George Aikens' saloon and Fleming's saloon and dance hall. On the south side, from west to east, were a Chinaman's (Charlie Signs') laundry, a small hut standing back from the road, the large Reynolds and Rath supply store, back of which was a hide yard, and, last, a hut occupied by James Knight, employed by Reynolds and Rath in the hide yard.

"Smokey" Thompson dug and filled a cistern with water in front of Aiken's saloon, and sold it to the hunters and others in town. He hauled water in barrels for his cistern from a creek a short distance north of Reynolds. The hunters and traders had to water their livestock in a common herd by driving to and from this creek twice a day.

Camp Reynolds had few attractions. Generally the

[18] Warren Pringle Moore to Carl Coke Rister, August 26, 1926; Naomi H. Kincaid, "Rath City," *West Texas Historical Association Year Book*, Vol. XXIV (October, 1948), 40ff.; R. C. Crane, "King of Them All," *Amarillo Sunday Globe-News*, August 14, 1938. At the present time this site is within the T-Diamond Ranch. Rath and Wright had been partners at Fort Elliott in 1874; Lee and Reynolds were Dodge City hide dealers.

air was filled with stench from stacked hides, which attracted swarms of insects. Squalor and filth were everywhere, since transient women cared as little for sanitation
as did their male companions. Saloon debauches, brawling,
and fights were common. In fact, Reynolds had its two-
grave boot hill, one the grave of "Spotted Jack," who was
reported to have been killed by Indians about one-half mile
north of town, and the other of Tom Lumpkins, who dueled
with Jim Smith in front of Aikens' saloon and lost.[19]

Twice a week mail was brought to Camp Reynolds
from Griffin, fifty miles away. At first cowboys brought it,
riding in relays from Griffin to the Caprock. Then James
W. Stell drove a stage from Griffin to Reynolds in the spring
of 1877, carrying mail and express.[20]

Camp Reynolds entertainment was as brutally raw as
its society. Both during the day and at night buffalo hunters, cowboys, and transients played cards, patronized the
bars, quarreled, and brawled. Occasionally a dance was
staged and all were invited to attend, including cowboys
from ranches far removed from Reynolds. On these occasions cowboys rode in and Fort Griffin girls also came,
"riding in big blue hide wagons." They danced throughout
the night to such fiddle melodies as "Turkey in the Straw"
and "Sally Goodins." It is small wonder that the dancing,
semiwild males went "calico minded" when they "got a
whiff of Hoyt's cologne."[21]

[19] Moore to Rister, August 26, 1926; James W. Stell to Rister, March
3, 1929.

[20] Pringle Moore, John R. Cook, and James W. Stell, all of whom
were at Reynolds during 1877–79, described the place as a primitive hide-
buying outpost. See Moore to Rister, August 26, 1926; Cook, *The Border
and the Buffalo* (Topeka, 1907), 190ff.; James W. Stell to Rister, March
3, 1929. See also Stell's letter to *Frontier Times*, Vol. VI (March, 1929),
215.

The Mooar brothers operated out of Fort Griffin. There they could not only purchase ammunition, food, and hunters' supplies, but also sell their smoked cuts of buffalo meat and tongue. On one occasion, on March 18, 1876, they sold to C. G. Convers and Company 164 buffalo tongues at 20 cents each, or a total of $32.60, and thirty pounds of smoked meat at six cents a pound, or $1.80. They sometimes realized more from these limited sales than their supplies cost them.[22] But they disposed of most of their flint hides at Fort Worth, instead of Dodge City, although all hide trains traveled via Griffin.

Meanwhile, at Dodge City, Rath and associates had sent their business manager, W. H. West, and their chief wagon master, General Russell, from Camp Reynolds to find a direct road to Griffin and to contact the Mooar brothers. In accomplishing the second part of their mission, they came to the Mooars' Haskell County camp in April, 1876, and bought 450 selected buffalo hides for delivery at the Cheyenne Agency, Indian Territory, which, in May, J. Wright Mooar delivered to Chief Whirlwind. While Mooar was there, he heard that seventy Comanches had broken out of their reservation and had gone to Texas. Black Beaver of the Wichita Agency warned him that in returning home he should "keep gun in one hand all time. Coat in wagon, two belt cartridges around waist in sight."[23] Mooar followed his instructions and arrived at Griffin in June without molestation by the runaway Indians.

John was ready to start eastward with a load of buffalo

[21] Kincaid, "Rath City," *West Texas Historical Association Year Book*, Vol. XXIV (October, 1948), 46.

[22] Itemized statement furnished by the merchant. See Mooar Papers.

[23] J. Wright Mooar, "Buffalo Days," *Holland's Magazine* (April, 1933), 22.

hides, and J. Wright rode a part of the way with him and then mounted his horse and completed his journey to Dallas. There he boarded a train for the East to visit his Vermont parents and to attend the Centennial Exposition at Philadelphia, while John sold the buffalo hides at Fort Worth, purchased supplies, and returned to Griffin.

When J. Wright returned, he found brother John camped on Foil Creek, four miles from Fort Griffin, with the Murphys, already loaded for the season's hunt. His outfit consisted of four nine-yoke teams of steers and thirteen wagons (some as trailers), and two four mule teams with two wagons each. John had employed nine men for the trip for teamsters, skinners, and general help. And after a two-day stay at Fort Griffin, the long train moved out toward the west to follow the divide between the Brazos and Colorado rivers to the buffalo range, traveling for a part of the way the military road, via Phantom Hill, toward Fort Concho. Beyond the site of present-day Sweetwater, the Mooars turned a bit north of west until on the morning of October 7, 1876, they came to a plain which was literally alive with buffalo. They made camp on Deep Creek,[24] in present Scurry County, the area of their future ranch. Here J. Wright bagged the now well-known white buffalo, the only one ever killed in Texas. The Mooars slew 4,500 buffalo in this area in four months and sold 2,000 pounds of meat at Fort Griffin at seven and one-half cents per pound.

They devised an interesting method for curing the meat. As soon as the hide was stripped from the fallen buffalo, four large pieces were cut from each ham (and others

[24] It was called Deep Creek, says Lydia Louise Mooar, when John exclaimed as he crossed it, "Well, this is a deep creek." See Lydia Louise Mooar, "Mooar Family," as cited, 19.

Ruins of Conrad's Store

from the hump), from which the bone had been taken. When from one thousand to twelve hundred pounds of meat was thus prepared, it was stacked in a vat made by driving four stakes in the ground, in a square four by four feet, the stakes standing four feet high. To these corner stakes was suspended a hide with its flesh side up and sagging in the middle to form a sack or vat to hold the meat. Brine was poured over the meat until it was covered. Then a second hide, flesh side down, was put over the meat to protect it from the sun, dust, and insects. Four days later sugar and saltpeter were added in equal quantity to the brine, and after two weeks the now thoroughly medicated meat was taken out and put in a smokehouse for final seasoning.

The Mooars made their smokehouse by stretching buffalo hides over a framework of hackberry poles, put together with eight-penny nails, one hundred pounds of which John had purchased in Fort Worth. The smokehouse was 110 feet long and 20 feet wide, within the floor-space of which had been dug ten square fire-pits, in which hackberry and chinaberry poles were burned. The smoke-curing process required ten or twelve days. Then the meat was sacked, loaded into wagons, and sold in Griffin and elsewhere. During the winter of 1877, 3,700 hides were sold in Fort Worth and 2,500 pounds of meat locally.[25]

About this time W. H. ("Pete") Snyder, a freighter with ox-teams, established a store on Deep Creek, where present-day Snyder, the county seat of Scurry County, now is. This became a new hide-buying center, which was presently visited by hundreds of hunters and wagon trains. McKaney and Hamburg had established a store at the head

---

[25] J. Wright Mooar, "Buffalo Days," *Holland's Magazine* (May, 1933), 12.

of the Clear Fork in Fisher County, west of present-day Roby. All these hide-buying and supply posts did a thriving business during the period, 1877–79.[26]

"Freighters are wanted to transport buffalo hides to Fort Worth," ran a Griffin news item in the fall of 1876. "The hunt is the largest ever known. Countless thousands of buffaloes cover the prairies. Ten thousand hides are now on the way to the railroad, and thousands await transportation to Fort Worth."[27] Nevertheless, the hides had started moving; the *Frontier Echo* of November 3, 1876, mentioned that a large wagon train loaded with buffalo hides had passed through Griffin that day at noon. Often freighters profited from a two-way business by hauling merchandise from Fort Worth wholesale houses to Griffin and returning to Fort Worth with buffalo hides.

Griffin now had the reputation of being the buffalo hunters' supply center and the best frontier market for flint hides. Many hunters lived there, where they had a base for frequent excursions into the buffalo country. Joe S. McCombs, John Jacobs, John Poe, Alex Howsley, and Jim Cardine, to mention only a few, were active Griffin hunters.

Back at Camp Reynolds, the hunters were plagued by Indian raids. About seventy-five Comanche warriors and their families had left the Wichita Mountains in southwestern Indian Territory and had sought an asylum in western Texas, their former choice buffalo hunting ground. The recent Sioux victory over Colonel George Custer's Seventh Cavalry at the Little Big Horn had encouraged them to leave their reservation. They would drive their white en-

[26] *Ibid.;* Lydia Louise Mooar, "Mooar Family," as cited, 19.
[27] *Fort Worth Democrat,* November 8, 1876.

emies, the buffalo hunters, from western Texas, for they were destroying the buffalo.

They left their Wichita Mountain home, led by a warrior whom the hunters knew only as "Nigger Horse," or "Black Horse," though contemporary records do not list a chief by that name.[28] Kiowa hunters had also moved southwest of their Rainy Mountain retreat to Elk Creek, a tributary of upper Red River, for Anko recorded on his calendar that he and other Kiowas hunted buffalo that winter.[29]

The runaway Comanches struck the hunters' hide camps like a thunderbolt. Late in February, 1877, they destroyed Billy Devins' camp, about forty-five miles west of Camp Reynolds, and stole his horses. Devins and his men barely escaped with their lives. On the same raid they descended on two Englishmen's camp while its owners were out hunting and burned their wagon and accumulated hides. About the same time Carr and Causey reported at Camp Reynolds that they had seen about fifty painted braves between the Double Mountain and Mackenzie Trail. Still later, eight hunters of Godey's camp were attacked, in which affray "Spotted Jack" was seriously wounded. While the others made their escape, "Spotted Jack" was left behind, hidden under an embankment, until his comrades could return with wagon and team to take him to Camp Reynolds. During his long hours of waiting, he became hungry and killed a buffalo, and cooked and ate a part of

[28] Any brave warrior could enlist volunteers for a raid; or the raiders, before leaving camp, could elect a warrior with prestige. Therefore the leader of this runaway band was not necessarily a chief. See Wallace and Hoebel, *The Comanches*, 250.

[29] Mooney, "Calendar History of the Kiowa Indians," *Seventeenth Annual Report of the Bureau of American Ethnology, 1895–96.*

it, which gave him enough strength to start for Camp Reynolds. While limping along, he met his friends returning with the wagon.[30]

Devins told the hunters, who were rapidly concentrating at Fort Reynolds, that Marshall Sewell might have been killed by the Quahadas; his camp was exposed to danger even more than his own. The aroused hunters quickly organized an armed band of eighteen men to go out to the camp, but before they reached it, "Wild Skillet" intercepted them, bringing the news that the Indians had killed Sewell, his employer, and had pillaged his camp. The hunters continued their journey to the dead man's camp, which they found burned. They also found Sewell's scalped and mutilated body, and buried it. The raiders had taken the dead man's .45 Creedmoor Sharps rifle and about seventy-five rounds of ammunition. Since nothing more could be done, the search party then returned to Camp Reynolds.

John R. Cook, W. S. Glenn, and "Moccasin Jim" (James W.) Stell, who were hide hunters at Camp Reynolds and members of an expedition against the Indians, tell generally the same story about their campaign, and differ only in

[30] Cook, *The Border and the Buffalo*, 291; Rex Strickland, ed., "The Recollections of W. S. Glenn, Buffalo Hunter," *Panhandle-Plains Historical Review*, Vol. XXII (1949), 46–47, 64. "Spotted Jack" lived to engage in the Pocket Canyon fight between the hunters and the Indians, according to Glenn. While O. W. Williams and other surveyors were camping about two miles north of Camp Reynolds, which he referred to as "Rath City," they heard shooting. Next morning, on August 12, 1877, they learned that "Spotted Jack" had been killed, but they could not learn by whom or why. See "From Dallas to the Site of Lubbock in 1877," *West Texas Historical Association Year Book*, Vol. XV (October, 1939), 20. See also *Galveston News*, March 30, 1877. A copy of this news item, as well as other material related to the Pocket Canyon fight, is found in L. B. Wood Papers, Breckenridge, Texas.

minor details. Cook and Glenn generally agreed about where they encountered and fought the Indians, with Glenn even naming the battle site as the Yellow House, "where the city of Lubbock now stands."[31]

Cook stated that one hundred men agreed to join the hunter force but that only forty-five—thirty horsemen and fifteen footmen—returned from the expedition. Glenn said that on the day before the fight, not counting their captain and lieutenant, there were forty-four. Frank Collinson, an English hunter with the expedition, stated that "there were four or five wagons loaded with camp supplies and corn for over sixty horses and mules; something over thirty men mounted and three or four on each wagon; also a full fifty-gallon barrel of whiskey." He further stated that "most of the outfit were fairly well 'loaded' when we started."[32]

This armed force left Camp Reynolds on March 1. Stell said that George West "furnished all the grub and we furnished our guns and ammunition, also 3 teams and wagons to carry our grub and bedding [instead of the "four or five" mentioned by Collinson], also with camp equipage, horse feed, medicines, splints, and bandages." Cook seemed disgusted because "fully 125 men had left the range going east, northeast, and southeast, into Henrietta, Phantom Hill and Fort Griffin country," some of whom had promised to join the expedition.

The hunters chose Hank Campbell as captain; Jim

31 Strickland, ed., "The Recollections of W. S. Glenn," *Panhandle-Plains Historical Review*, Vol. XXII (1949), 44ff. Stell wrote that they found "the Comanches at the head of the Double Mountain Fork," and later in his letter, "We went into the canyon just below the Yellow House bluff. They were taking their teepees down." Steel to Rister, March 3, 1929.

32 Frank Collinson, "The Battle of Yellow House Draw," *Ranch Romances* (July, 1935), 146.

Smith, second in command; and Joe Freed, third—but none of them had had military experience.[33] José Tafoya, referred to by the hunters as "Hosea" and "Hozay," and reported to be one of Mackenzie's former scouts, acted as their trailer. Each day their little army traveled slowly, and it was not until March 17 that it was in striking distance of the south prong of the Yellow House. When it reached the Caprock, it turned southward for a short distance, looking for a place to ascend to the Staked Plains. The scout found a steep ascent, probably not far from the present town of Post, where by doubling teams and by the footmen pushing, one by one the wagons were hauled up to the high plain and the journey was continued, paralleling Yellow House Canyon. While cautiously advancing, an English hide hunter came upon and killed a Quahada "sign-rider," or scout, and hid his body in the rank tules growing along the Yellow House Creek. Near midnight José found the Indian village on the south fork of the Yellow House about three and one-half miles above its junction with the north fork, or above present Mackenzie Park.

After considerable maneuvering and planning, the

[33] Glenn said that the hunters composing the expedition were Captain Jim Harvey, José Tafoya, Dick Wilkinson, "Spotted Jack" Dean, Bill Benson, "Mexican Joe," "Squirrel Eye" Charly Emory, "Limpy" Jim Smith, Hank Campbell, Sol Reese, Bill Kress, Bill Belden, John Whaley, "Sixshooter" Bill Hillman, "Scorpion" Jack, "Hurricane" Lee Grimes, Tom Hogler, Doc Neil, Frank Hinton, B. F. Daniels, "Hi" Bickerdyke, Louis Keyes, "Whiskey" Jim Greathouse, George Cornett, Harry Forest, "Big Beans," "Smokey" Thompson, Ed O'Byrne (?), Paten (interpreter), George Holmes, John Cook, Mack Matthias, "Slap Jack Bill," Bill Nay, Alfred Waite, "Hog" Jim Smith, and Bill Milligan. Strickland, ed., "The Recollections of W. S. Glenn, Buffalo Hunter," *Panhandle-Plains Historical Review*, Vol. XXII (1949), 64. The narratives of other hunters have the names of participants not included in this list.

hunters, divided into three bands, attacked the village in the early morning of March 18. When the horsemen riding down the creek came in sight of the first tipis, they met the warriors running toward them, having poured out of their tipis, leaving their women and children to escape as best they could. The hunters were surprised to find that the Indians outnumbered them about two to one, for upwards of one hundred New Mexico Apaches (Mescaleros), and doubtless *Comancheros*, were trading at the village. They joined the Comanches in the fight,[34] but shortly fled back to New Mexico.

Eight days after the fight, one of the hunter participants returned to Dodge City and gave the local editor an account of it. He said that during the night of March 17 the advancing hunters came to a Blanco Canyon camping ground which the Indians had recently abandoned, five or six miles below present-day Lubbock. "For forty-eight hours," he said, "they had traveled without food, but the evident close proximity to the objects of their hate fired them with new zeal and added fresh vigor to their gaunt, attenuated frames. If the noble red man could have witnessed the terrible earnestness with which on this evening the hunters pledged themselves neither to eat nor sleep until the mutilated remains of Marshal Sewell had been tenfold avenged, they would not have slumbered quite so serenely as they did. All night long the party pressed wearily and painfully forward.[35]

[34] The *Fort Griffin Echo,* April 27, 1877, carried a *San Antonio Herald* news item saying that buffalo hunters had pursued and overtaken thieves 150 miles northwest of Fort Concho, and that in a battle which followed they had killed "three Indians, two Mexicans, and one white man." But it was silent on the Pocket Canyon fight.

[35] Paragraphing is changed here for easier reading.

183

"When the day dawned they had traveled about twelve miles. A little after sunup a sight met their view which lit up their haggard and unshaven countenances with demoniac glee. On the banks of a small stream a short distance ahead they saw a band of Indian warriors and squaws—the hostile Apaches who had murdered, scalped, and plundered their friends.

"The Indians at first seemed inclined to retreat, but soon discovered the comparatively small number of whites and concluded to take the offensive. The first shots were fired by the Indians. The hunters did not appear to realize the fact that the Indians numbered fully twice their strength, they were equally well armed and in good fighting condition. They only knew that the time to fulfill their vows of vengeance was at hand. The days of weary pursuit and gnawing hunger were forgotten. . . . Some of them [the hunters] were severely wounded, but they laughed at their pain, and their aim was more deadly than before. The Indians soon began to realize that their boldest braves were being shot down, and their enemies becoming more bloodthirsty at every volley, they therefore retreated to a more sheltered locality. The hunters followed and all day long the firing was kept up. Every time a brave exposed his person to get a shot at the hunters that same daring brave would start on his trip to the happy hunting grounds of his forefathers.

"When the shades of evening draped the scene of carnage, in the morning," concluded the *News* article, "the Apaches gathered up their dead and silently stole away, leaving gore enough to fully quench the hunters' thirst for revenge. The number of killed and wounded Indians could not be ascertained. Only a few hunters were wounded and none killed."[36] Actually, the hunters had ended the fight. Their ammunition was almost exhausted and they were in need of food and water; consequently, Campbell hurriedly broke off the fight and began his retreat down the canyon with the Indians close on his heels. Early next morning his men fired the grass behind them, and the billowing, dense smoke, borne on an east wind, screened their withdrawal. No doubt, too, the warriors were pleased with their withdrawal; they did not follow them below the Caprock.

The excited hide hunters had gone for many hours without rest or food, so that evening, while encamped below the Caprock, supper was enjoyed by all. Cook stated that they opened two boxes of crackers, carved a big cheese, made two camp kettles of oyster soup, opened peach cans by the dozen, set out pickles, made strong coffee, and sat down to a feast.[37]

They also had time to look after their wounded. José's shoulder wound was probed, washed, sprinkled with iodoform, and bandaged; splints were made for Grimes's broken wrist, caused by a nasty spill from his horse during the battle; and Joe Jackson's serious groin wound was treated, but without too much success. A warrior, armed with Sewell's Sharps, had shot him. He was so seriously wounded that he was carried in a wagon. Later, he was sent to the Fort Griffin hospital, where he died two months later, after

[36] *Dodge City Times*, May 26, 1877. The *Galveston News*, April 5, 1877, also carried an account of the "Pocket Canyon" fight which in general coincided with the *Times* narrative. See also Frank Collinson to Bruce Gerdes, December 16, 1937 (MS in Wood Papers, Breckenridge, Texas). Collinson was quite elderly at the time he wrote this letter, which reveals his pronounced prejudice against John R. Cook and his *The Border and the Buffalo*. Yet his own account in some respects is much like Cook's, but generally less trustworthy.
[37] Cook, *The Border and the Buffalo*, 232.

the post surgeon had extracted the heavy lead bullet causing the wound. The hunters returned to Camp Reynolds on March 22.[38]

The Indian warriors followed the hunters back to Camp Reynolds, but generally far enough behind to keep out of rifle range. They also attacked the camps of hunters yet in the field, Bickerdyke and Benson lost eight head of stock from their camp forty miles northwest of Reynolds; Glenn and two Englishmen, sixty miles west, were attacked (Glenn was wounded), their wagons were destroyed, twenty-two hundred rounds of ammunition were taken, and seven head of stock were run off.

On the night of May 1 the warriors boldly raided Camp Reynolds and captured twenty-five horses.[39] John Cook, Louie Keyes, George Cornett, "Squirrel Eye" (Charlie Emory), "Hi" Bickerdyke, Joe Freed, and Jim Harvey were returning from John Sharp's hide camp near Double Mountain with Sharp, who had been wounded by the Indians. The Indians had plundered Sharp's camp, cut the spokes out of his wagon wheels, and run off his team. Before they reached Reynolds, they saw the Indians "going west to beat h–l, driving over 100 head of horses." Cook said that when he and his party reached Reynolds, they met a cheap-looking crowd of about fifty men. The Indians had made a clean job of the raid. The hunters planned a reprisal raid, but they presently learned that the Indians had broken up into small bands to operate along the extended border.[40]

Meanwhile, Fort Griffin cavalry was sent westward to

[38] *Ibid.*

[39] The *Dodge City Times,* June 2, 1877, reported that the raiders had "captured twenty-five head of stock which Frank Foster was herding nearby."

[40] Cook, *The Border and the Buffalo,* 241–42, 245.

break up Comanche and Mescalero pillaging. Captain P. L. Lee left that post on the morning of April 19, 1877, with Company G (forty-two men) of the Tenth Cavalry, five wagons, ten pack mules, and ten Tonkawa scouts headed by Chief Johnson. When he arrived at Flat Top Mountain (a mesa) a few miles northeast of the present-day Hamlin, Texas, he sent two wagons, a corporal, and two men with eight days' rations for another detachment of his cavalry at Big Spring. He and this detachment were to scout about Blanco Canyon, Casa Amarilla, and the lakes Sabinas, Sulphur Springs, and Mustang Springs. He had heard that Indians were at or near these places.

Meanwhile, Lee's own command moved from Flat Top to Blanco Canyon, where he arrived on April 28 and established a camp. From there he scouted up the canyon to its head without seeing Indians, and then he returned to his camp and sent three wagons back to Fort Griffin for supplies. On the next day he found a trail of twelve or fifteen Indians in the Yellow House Canyon. He was convinced, however, that these Indians had come from their village, since the trail indicated that they had "no stock except that which they were riding." He decided to follow the trail to the village and destroy it.

Accordingly, Lee backtracked the trail, following it to a camp site at Laguna Agua Negra, recently abandoned. There he found a "number of Caretta [*carreta* or cart] tracks leading to and from it," showing that *Comancheros* had been there recently with supplies for the Indians.

He continued to follow the trail on May 4 and found the Indians camped at Lake Quemada, west of Silver Lake, in the northern part of present Cochran County. About 2:00 P. M. the Tonk scouts signaled that the village was in sight. "I charged into it," Lee reported to the Fort Griffin adjutant, and in the fight which ensued four Indians were killed, and two children and four women were captured.[41] Most of the warriors were away from the village hunting buffalo. Lee did not say what band of Indians this was, but the accounts of hunters who were in the "Pocket Canyon" fight list them as the same Comanches and Apaches whom they had recently attacked.

The *Dodge City Times* of June 2, 1877, announced that Lee had returned to Camp Reynolds on May 10 "with four scalps, six squaws, and forty head of ponies." Cook learned of Lee's Lake Quemada fight at Fort Griffin. He had gone to the hospital there with a hunter who had suffered a broken arm in a Camp Reynolds saloon brawl. Then, after he had returned to Reynolds, while he and about twenty-five hunters were lounging around Rath's store and saloon, Lee's command came in with their Indian prisoners.[42] He told the hunters, Cook said, that they had killed thirty-one warriors in the "Pocket Canyon" fight and had so severely wounded four others that they died the next day. The hunters had previously thought that they had killed about twelve.[43]

From Reynolds, Lee journeyed on to Fort Griffin, where he reported to the commanding officer that he had captured from the Indians a large quantity of powder,

[41] Lee's "Report to the Fort Griffin Adjutant, May 25, 1877" (MS, Division of War Records, National Archives, Washington); Richard G. Wood to Carl Coke Rister, March 21, 1955. See also "Medical History of the Post, Fort Griffin, Texas, 1867–81," as cited, particularly the entries for April and May, 1877; Heitman, *Historical Register and Dictionary*, II, 443.

[42] Cook, *The Border and the Buffalo*, 235–36. Lee's report to the Fort Griffin adjutant substantiated Cook's account of the Lake Quemada fight.

[43] *Ibid.*

lead, dried meat, blankets, robes, and several rifles and revolvers.[44]

Captain D. G. Caldwell, assistant surgeon at Fort Griffin, reported that Captain Lee returned to Fort Griffin on May 13, 1877, announced the death of Sergeant Charles Butler of Company G, Tenth Cavalry, "in a skirmish with the Comanche Indians at Laguna Quemada."[45] Cook's narrative added other details. He wrote that Captain Lee found the Indians camping at *Laguna Plata* (probably the *Laguna Quemada* which Lee reported). Chief Johnson and four of his tribesmen had followed their trail from the Yellow House camp site to their new village while most of the warriors were out hunting. Lee engaged those left behind in a skirmish, in which, wrote Cook, Lee's "first duty sergeant" (Charles Butler) had been killed "by old Nigger Horse himself." At the same time "the sergeant killed both Nigger Horse and his squaw, as they were trying to make their escape, both mounted upon one pony."[46] Five other warriors were also killed in a running fight "toward the Blue sand hills."

At Fort Griffin, McCombs, Jacobs, and Poe had rigged up their first buffalo hunt about Christmas, 1874, traveling westward over the Mackenzie Trail and into Haskell County.[47] They established their camp at Mocking Bird Springs, six or seven miles northeast of present-day Haskell. The hunters realized that they were exposed to Indian attack, but they believed that their long-range guns would keep their foes at a distance. There was no house or settle-

[44] Lee's "Report to the Fort Griffin Adjutant, May 25, 1877," as cited.

[45] "Medical History of the Post, Fort Griffin, 1867–81," as cited, particularly the entries for April and May, 1877.

[46] Cook, *The Border and the Buffalo*, 238.

[47] "Frontier Life of Uncle Joe S. McCombs," as cited.

ment west of the Old Stone Ranch, so the vast rangelands of Shackelford and Throckmorton counties were yet grazed by thousands of buffalo.

McCombs did all the killing and Poe and Jacobs the skinning. Like all professional buffalo hunters, they employed well-known formulas in taking and curing hides. McCombs would start their work. He would steal upon a herd of peacefully grazing bison and select a vantage point, within easy range of the animals, where he could hide himself. Then he would begin shooting, resting his gun on a "rest stick" or tripod. "I would always shoot the leader of the herd, generally a bull," he later wrote.[48] When it fell, the other bison would mill about until another bull assumed the leadership and started a stampede. But before this could happen, the hidden marksmen would often have time to kill twenty-five or fifty animals in the herd.

The skinners were equally skillful. Whenever possible, experienced hunters made haste to skin a fallen buffalo before *rigor mortis* set in; and at all hazards, before they should become hard frozen, for one skinner could skin a warm animal single-handed, whereas two were ordinarily required if the bison were frozen stiff. In this methodical work the skinner used two knives, which he sharpened frequently on a whetstone or sharpening steel, one a "ripping-knife" and the other a "skinning-knife." He generally carried a pritch stick, with a sharp nail in one end. With it, he could prop up, feet upward, the carcass by catching its tough hide with the nail.

Sometimes the skinners employed an ox- or mule-

[48] *Ibid.* "The young cow and spikes" (young bulls) were best for meat and robes. Hides of old bulls were tanned and used for such heavy leather as belting. Their meat was coarse and tough.

drawn wagon to assist them. John R. Cook thus described this expedited procedure: "We fastened a forked stick to the center of the hind axle-tree of a wagon, letting the end drag on the ground, on an incline to say 20 degrees; fastened a chain or rope to the same axle, then we would drive up quartering to the carcass and hook the loose end of the chain over a front leg. After skinning the upper side down, then start the team up and pull the dead animal up a little, and stop. (The stick prevented the wagon from backing up). Then we would skin the belly down to the backbone, and the hide was separated from the carcass. We would then throw the hide in the wagon, and proceed as before until all the hides were skinned from the dead carcasses."[49]

The term "flint hide" was derived from the flint-like stiffness of the hide when once it was cured and ready for shipment. When it was first stripped from the dead animal, the hunter stretched it upon the ground, flesh side up, and drove about fourteen pegs in its edges. After three or four days, the pegs would be pulled and it would be turned over with the flesh side down. Then every other day it would be turned again until it was dry and hard. When all the dry hides were ready for market, they were folded lengthwise and stacked. Then thongs were cut from a green hide, tied in pegholes of the bottom and uppermost hides and drawn tightly and tied. This bale and others similarly prepared were now ready for hauling.[50]

The Griffin hunters had a profitable season. McCombs reported that after a few weeks he, Poe, and Jacobs finally moved from their Haskell base. They came down to the

[49] Cook, *The Border and the Buffalo*, 116–17.
[50] W. C. Holden, "The Buffalo of the Plains Area," *West Texas Historical Association Year Book*, Vol. II (June, 1926), 14.

Clear Fork and headed up that stream, via Phantom Hill, to a site near present-day Rotan, in Fisher County. There they stayed until May, 1875, and got 1,300 hides. Their season's kill at both camps, McCombs said, was 2,000 bison, the hides of which they sold to Conrad and Rath at Griffin for $2.00 for each robe hide and $1.50 for the others.[51] These hides were the first of any consequence which were marketed in Griffin.

In the following fall, McCombs, Poe, and Jacobs made their third hunt, employing Bob Pitcock, Sol Pace, and Wesley Tarter as skinners. They hauled in their mule-drawn wagon eight hundred pounds of lead and five kegs of powder, McCombs' Sharps sporting rifle, and his reloading outfit. Almost all experienced hunters carried their own cartridge reloading equipment.

Again the hunters moved up the Clear Fork via Phantom Hill to Fisher County and then southward to approximately the site of present-day Sweetwater. Here they gleaned several hundred hides before moving on westward to Champion Creek south of what is today Colorado City, Texas. There they made permanent camp until April 1. McCombs' total season's bag was 2,000 buffalo. Upon his return to Griffin he sent back to his hunting camp five or six wagons for them, each with a trailer, and each pulled by six yoke of oxen.

His next hunting trip was also profitable. By the fall of 1876, northern hunters were invading in great numbers his recently found hunting area, and their big guns could be heard booming ceaselessly. But McCombs was unconcerned about their proximity. His party made camp on Morgan Creek over the divide west of present Colorado

[51] "Frontier Life of Uncle Joe S. McCombs," as cited.

Early-day sketch of Fort Griffin,
reproduced from a letterhead in official records
of Adjutant General Department, Texas.
This is the only known likeness
of the Fort Griffin post.

City. Their season's hides taken were 2,300, a part of which he sold for $1.00 each to a visiting dealer, and the others at Griffin for $1.50 each.

In September, 1877, he again left Griffin, this time on his most successful hunt, taking several skinners, a Mexican to peg down the hides, and one thousand pounds of lead and five kegs of powder. For a short time he camped at the Big Spring, near where is now situated a thriving young city by that name. Then he moved to Mossy Rock Springs near Signal Mountain, ten miles south of Big Spring. On this trip he made his biggest kill, 4,900 buffalo; his neighbors, the Poe and Jacobs party, killed 6,300. Two other hunting outfits stacked hides they had acquired at his camp, and at one time the three groups had 9,700 hides in this temporary yard. W. H. Webb of Dallas bought them for $1.00 each, camp delivery.

McCombs' last hunt, in 1878, was near Mustang Pond, on the site of Midland, Texas, where he killed only 800 buffalo. The great Southern herd had diminished almost to the vanishing point. In later years, McCombs estimated that he had slain 12,000 buffalo during his several hunting trips in western Texas.[52]

Camp Reynolds' prosperity passed with the buffalo-hide industry's decline. Stell said that he did not know how many hides Rath and associates bought during more than two years of this hide town's existence, "but it was close to a million." And this was not all. The Camp Reynolds buyers could not haul all the huge accumulation of hides; therefore, long bull trains from Denison and Fort Worth moved them eastward to market via Griffin. In 1879, when remnants of the great herd ceased to visit the Double Moun-

[52] *Ibid.*

tain area and moved farther south, Camp Reynolds and
other temporary hide camps on Deep Creek and in Fisher
County were deserted by the men who made them.

But Griffin lingered on. It was still the most advanced
buffalo town, where hunters could exchange meat and
hides for guns, ammunition, and other supplies; it yet enjoyed a large volume of trade with the trail drivers. Its
streets, saloons, and dives yet afforded diversion to all
visitors seeking dangerous excitement and entertainment.
Desperate outlaws, the scum of the West, were drawn to
the Flat because of its "resounding reputation." Along with
Deadwood and Dodge City it had an unenviable record,
the habitat of the mammoth of violence. It drew hard-
visaged and cold-eyed lawmen and killers, the way un-
sightly garbage draws flies. Its undesirables, such as "Hurricane" Bill, "Doc" Holliday, and "Big Nose" Kate, at least
temporarily, kept alive its drawing power. Such lawmen as
Wyatt Earp and Pat Garrett were familiar figures on the
streets and in the dives, for here they found desperate killers, gamblers, and thieves. Earp came to enlist the services
of Holliday to run down and arrest the notorious Dave
Rudabaugh; Pat Garrett rode in from the west, where he
had encountered questionable characters at Camp Reynolds,[53] but he did not state what his mission was.

Both the wild cowboys and hide hunters found the
Flat a hard town. Stell wrote that "they [there] were 30
men kill[ed] around Fort Griffin in the month of April,
'77," although his information was probably rumor more
than fact.[54] He was a sober frontiersman, but knew where

[53] John Myers, *Doc Holliday* (Boston and Toronto, 1955), 65ff.
[54] Stell to Rister, March 3, 1929.

to find the Flat's principal cesspools, like the Bee Hive Saloon and the Mexican dance hall and saloon down near the river, "where the nigger troops would come."

The proportions of Griffin's hide industry was portrayed by articles appearing in the *Fort Worth Democrat*. Bill Akers of Griffin wrote in January, 1877, that sixteen hundred hide hunters were on the buffalo range, most of whom received their supplies at Griffin. In May, he reported that "one train of ten wagons came in yesterday morning. In front were eleven yoke of oxen, driven by one man, and dragging after them four large new wagons, heavily laden. Two other teams, with seven yokes each, drawing three wagons, followed," the train carrying from 2,500 to 3,000 hides. In August, about 200,000 hides changed hands in Griffin, and were from there freighted to railway shipping points. In January, 1878, a Griffin four-acre hide yard was covered with hides spread out to dry. Wagon trains were continually going and coming. They had already handled 20,000 hides for the season. During this year another paper estimated that two thousand hide men were destroying the Southern herd at the rate of 200,-000 annually, operating over a "grand circuit of hundreds of miles."[55]

Such a volume of business brought new enterprises to Griffin. The *Fort Worth Democrat* of January 9, 1878, indicated that John Swartz's Planters House was still a popular hotel. It had two stories, seventeen rooms, and new furniture. The new establishments listed were Guss's saloon, the biggest in town, Julius Hervey's restaurant,

[55] *Fort Worth Democrat*, January 25, May 3, August 4, 1877, and January 3, 1878; *Fort Worth Standard*, January 4, 1878.

George D. Baker and Dave de Long's Variety Theater, James Murphy's barbershop, and J. M. Cupp and Brother's and Henry Hamburg's stores.

Then by summer came the noticeable business lag, caused in large part by the hide industry's decline. In February a *Democrat* reporter interviewed buffalo hunters on Griffin's Main Street. They said that "the hunt had been much smaller than during the previous season, and that the buffalo seemed to have moved northward out of Texas."[56]

Griffin merchants tried frantically to continue the boom by making liberal exchanges with the hunters, for they had high hopes of drawing the Texas and Pacific Railroad by their town. Meanwhile, they would do several times more business than both of Griffin's rivals, Albany and Breckenridge. Indicative of this was Conrad's advertisements of tanned buffalo robes for sale,[57] and, in the next month, of shipping out a "wagon load of furs, two of deer and antelope skins, and four of beef hides." Etta Soule said that a local tannery turned out excellent rugs and laprobes,[58] and merchants kept households supplied with smoked sweet and juicy buffalo meat and tongue.

But all these business efforts were for naught; Griffin's rapid decline came in a matter of several months. By the fall of 1879 the Southern herd had been destroyed.

[56] *Fort Worth Democrat,* February 5, 1878.
[57] *Fort Griffin Echo,* January 17, 1880.
[58] "Fort Griffin as Seen through the Telescope of Memory," in Soule Papers (MS, Robert Nail Collection, Albany, Texas).

X   Toward Oblivion

A RAPID SETTLEMENT of the Fort Griffin country by ranchers and farmers came during the late 1870's. In fact, much of Texas' frontier had advanced westward, at some points fifty miles or more, either because of the building of railroads or because of an ever increasing influx of immigrants. Several of the border forts, including Fort Griffin, were well within the settled areas and were no longer needed. The once hostile Comanche and Kiowa Indians were now peacefully established on their Indian Territory reservation, learning how "to walk on the white man's road."

So at sundown, on May 31, 1881, the United States flag flying above Fort Griffin was lowered for the last time, and Captain J. B. Irvine, with Company A, Twenty-second Infantry, marched southward to Fort Clark, leaving Fort Griffin to oblivion.[1]

The Flat's abandonment was hardly so sudden. Almost three years earlier Editor Robson had grudgingly admitted that business was dull, "because all the merchants say so."[2]

[1] *Fort Griffin Echo*, June 4, 1881.   [2] *Ibid.*, October 11, 1878.

Several factors contributed to this lag in sales. The county seat of Albany was claiming a part of the trail drivers' trade, and was to capture the most of it within a few years. No longer could Fort Griffin give strong support to the Flat's merchants. In the early 1870's, when the post contained three hundred or more officers and enlisted men, much of their trade went to the Flat; but for the last several years only one company of infantry or cavalry had been stationed there. And now the fort was abandoned. The fast-declining buffalo meat and hide industries had been more catastrophic, for during the years 1874–78 merchants and buyers alike had money. But by 1879 the hide hunters had returned to their homes.

Curiously enough, railroad-building in western Texas had affected Griffin adversely. Griffin promoters had high hopes that the Texas and Pacific, building westward from Fort Worth, would pass through their town. These hopes were blasted, however, when it became known that the road's management had elected the Weatherford, Ranger, Eastland, Cisco, and Baird route. Abilene, a Texas and Pacific tent town, thirty-six miles southwest of Albany, arose overnight. Then Griffin sought the Texas Central Railroad, incorporated as a subsidiary of the Houston and Texas Central. It was building northwestward from Waco via Cisco. But Albany made its bid in a material way, and won, by raising a $50,000 bonus. Its victory was celebrated by the arrival of the first train on December 20, 1881, and Griffin was left holding the snipe-hunter's bag.[3]

Editor Robson was in the doldrums, for already an exodus had started. The town's "tainted beauties," together

[3] Grant, "The Early History of Shackelford County," as cited, 145 ff.; *Fort Griffin Echo*, January 7, 1880.

with their consorts, the saloon proprietors, barkeepers, gamblers, and transient opportunists, were leaving, much to the delight of the substantial citizens; but better-class businessmen were also either leaving or watching apprehensively the rapid appearance of tent towns along the two railroads.

In January, 1880, Robson took inventory of his town.[4] Among the prominent business enterprises, he first listed Conrad and Rath on Government Hill. But these two partners had already arrived at a business separation agreement. Rath was soon to depart for Dodge City, where he had other interests. Conrad had recently bought the Flat's Wichita Saloon building, and his carpenters and painters were "busily engaged in altering, enlarging, and beautifying" it to receive a $40,000 stock of goods.[5] These merchants had enjoyed an almost exclusive trade with the buffalo hunters and cowboys, notwithstanding the fact that F. B. York and Company carried a varied stock of merchandise valued at $20,000 to $25,000.

Robson also listed other miscellaneous businesses, including J. M. Cupp and Brother, groceries and hardware; the saloons of J. H. Chanssey, Charley Meyers, and Gus Huber; the hotels, boardinghouses, and restaurants of John Swartz, William Wilson, George Soule (who also operated a stage line), and Ben Volino. That is, Ben had a restaurant until "misfortune in the shape of a large crowd of buffalo hunters had swooped down upon him like an avalanche," after which, "Ben was not numbered among the solid men of the land." Still he remained "cheerful and plucky."

Then there were other individual operators. Pete Hav-

[4] *Ibid.*, January 31, 1880.
[5] *Fort Griffin Echo*, October 18, 1878.

erty managed a livery stable and wagon yard; J. F. Boze-
man, served as postmaster and kept a news and stationery
shop and, across the street, a feed and wagon yard; E.
Chiflet, owned the only tannery in town, and, indeed, in
Northwest Texas; Stribling and Sears were land agents;
Louis Wolfrom, proprietor of a bakery, stable, and wagon
yard; Dr. R. B. Lignoske, the town's only druggist; and
Elizah Earls, a town barber.

The Flat's professional men included Dr. I. J. Culver
and Dr. M. W. Powell; County Attorney J. N. Browning;
County Julge C. K. Stribling, Judge M. D. Kent, and Judge
J. W. Wray—all of whom "enjoyed fair practice."

Among the Flat's early hotels was the wooden, two-
story Occidental, built and, for a time, operated by "Uncle
Hank" Smith, or Hans Schmidt.[6] Don H. Biggers said that
"Aunty Smith" was cook, and "Uncle Hank" dishwasher,
office man, roustabout, and diplomat. He was "a grand success in dealing with drunks and other peace disturbers." He
was also a linguist, speaking English, German, Spanish, and
at least four Indian languages.[7]

[6] Hans Schmidt was born in Bavaria, Germany, August 15, 1836. His
parents died while he was a child and he came to America with his sister.
He attended school some, worked on a Lake Erie boat, and then as a bull-
whacker had a wagon train bound for Santa Fé. Later, he joined another
emigrant train for California, where he worked in the gold mines. He then
returned via the Southern Trail to El Paso and fought Indians in Arizona
and New Mexico, and from there joined other Californians to work in
mines in Mexico. At the outbreak of the Civil War he joined the Southern
army and served as a dispatcher, and after the war, as an interpreter at
El Paso. In 1872, he went to Griffin, where he met and married Elizabeth
Boyle. See John R. Hutto, "Mrs. Elizabeth (Aunt Hank) Smith," *West
Texas Historical Association Year Book,* Vol. XV (October, 1939), 46;
Hattie M. Anderson, "Mining and Indian Fighting in Arizona and New
Mexico, 1858–1861: Memoirs of Hank Smith," *Panhandle-Plains His-
torical Review,* Vol. I (1928), 67.

During Biggers' boyhood his father occasionally brought him from his Stephens County home to Griffin for extended visits with "Uncle Hank" and "Aunty," who treated him as if he were their son. Biggers yet remembers an experience at the Occidental, which he refers to as the Smith Hotel. In the latter part of 1868 a new hack, drawn by a pair of fine-blooded bay horses, drew up before the hotel. Its occupants were a liveried driver and a well-dressed man and woman. Following the hack were several wagons, loaded with provisions and supplies, particularly "good wines, whiskies, and cigars." Charles Tasker owned this small caravan.

Tasker announced to any and all persons that he was looking for a buffalo ranch. He was well supplied with cash. Among those who heard his surprising announcement were gamblers and sharpers who were equally adept at selling "gold bricks" and at card playing. But here indeed was an astonishing "sucker," the juiciest plum that had yet fallen to them, for Tasker had boasted that he was a gambling expert. Co-operating locals sought to give him opportunities to prove his skill.

"Then," Biggers wrote, "things began to happen."[7] The financing end of Tasker's venture got suspicious and investigated. Result: his allowance was discontinued. His funds were exhausted, and he still owed large sums to Conrad and Rath, the Occidental, and others in town.

In addition, he had employed Hank Smith to build a two-story house on his newly acquired ranch in Blanco Canyon, Crosby County, not far from the present town of Crosbyton. Its walls were of native stone. An Irishman by

[7] Biggers to Miss Etta Soule, December 16, 1944 (MS in Soule Papers–Robert Nail Collection, Albany, Texas).

the name of McGuire burned the lime in a near-by quarry, and the lumber for flooring, door and window frames, ceiling, and roof was hauled from Fort Worth at a freight charge of $90 per hundred pounds.[8]

As though the loss of all his ready cash was not enough, Tasker was bulldozed, threatened, and terrorized by a tough character whom he had hired as a ranch foreman. "Finally," Biggers wrote, "desperate, scared, and disgusted, Tasker deeded his land, with all improvements," including the house, four sections of land, rock barn, and corral to "Uncle Hank" Smith in lieu of money he owed him; and one dark night he and his wife were piloted out of the country by a young ranch hand. "Uncle Hank" considered the ranch a bad deal at $500, the amount Tasker owed him, but he accepted it and moved from Griffin out to it.[9]

When the Smiths had time to adjust themselves at the Blanco Canyon ranch, they were delighted. Hank wrote optimistically to Editor Robson and other friends at Griffin. He urged them to come out for a visit, if they desired profitable hunting and fishing. They could indulge in these sports to their hearts' content. The canyon stream was filled with fish. "We can show you more of them, large ones, and varieties innumerable," he exulted, "than can be found in any country on earth. Come and bring your fishing and hunting outfits—we will furnish all other necessities, including 'red liquor.' "

Hunters could still find buffalo. In the spring Smith expected to corral buffalo calves and start a herd of his own, thus realizing Tasker's earlier dream. He believed, too, that

[8] Hutto, "Mrs. Elizabeth (Aunt Hank) Smith," *West Texas Historical Association Year Book*, Vol. XV (October, 1939), 43–44.
[9] Biggers to Soule, September 16, 1944.

it was an excellent place for hogs, for he had killed yearling shoats which weighed nearly three hundred pounds each, and they had not eaten a kernel of grain. He also said that the canyon, within a mile of his house, could supply five thousand tons of hay, which showed that this was real cow country.[10]

"Aunty Hank" said later that their nearest neighbors were on the Reid ranch near Double Mountain in Stonewall County. Her first woman neighbor was Mrs. Dockum, who came from New York. She lived on a ranch near Spur, about twenty-five miles east of the Blanco Canyon ranch; presently another was Mrs. H. H. Campbell, whose husband was manager of the Matador property. And shortly a colony of Quakers settled at Estacado.[11]

Fort Griffin, 175 miles distant, was the Smiths' nearest post office, and for many months they seldom received any mail, only when cowboys distributed it to the scattered ranches. Then federal postal authorities granted them a post office, named Mount Blanco. "Aunty Hank" said, "I was appointed the first postmaster. I held the office from 1879 till 1916." She said that they were still dependent on Griffin; she had to go back there to have Frank Conrad and Si Able sign her bond.[12]

The beginning of Griffin's business recession came at a critical time. Other border towns were offering stiff trade competition. But Griffin for a time could claim established trade connections and other advantages, one of which was that it was a staging center. In 1877, C. Bain and Company

[10] *Frontier Echo,* December 6, 1878.

[11] Hutto, "Mrs. Elizabeth (Aunt Hank) Smith," *West Texas Historical Association Year Book,* Vol. XV (October, 1939), 44. Other Griffin settlers presently followed the Smiths out to Caprock country.

[12] *Ibid.,* 45.

was operating a stagecoach service from Weatherford to Jacksboro, Fort Belknap, and Griffin, and return. While visiting in Jacksboro, Bain announced that he was putting on this line new coaches from Concord, New Hampshire.[13]

Two years later Frank Conrad advertised daily mail and passenger services (except Sunday) of stages to and from Albany, Graham, Fort Concho, Fort Elliott, and Mount Blanco. George Soule operated the mail hack to Fort Concho.[14]

Griffin also had cultural advantages. At the opera house occasional stage plays could be enjoyed. And on Sundays townsmen and Clear Fork settlers, coming on horseback, in wagons, hacks, and buggies, attended religious services; in summers, Baptist and Methodist ministers preached in camp meeting for ten days or two weeks at a time to revive the drooping spirits of those whom Griffin's bright lights had at one time lured. Also sinners were ardently called to repentance—even the Flat's most dangerous characters.

The settlers had always given steadfast support to the education of their children, in the early 1880's maintaining the Fort Griffin Academy, whose principal was William S. Dalrymple, a schoolman highly respected for his ability. The schoolhouse was a stone structure which had escaped the vandalism soon to ravish the buildings on Government Hill and in the Flat. It was a two-story building, the upper floor devoted to Masonic Lodge work, and the lower to school purposes. Miss Etta Soule, one of W. S. Dalrymple's star pupils, remembered in later years the thoroughness of the instruction given her. Dalrymple was the principal, and

[13] *Frontier Echo*, February 23, 1877.
[14] *Fort Griffin Echo*, November 15, 1879, and January 10, 1880.

his sister-in-law, Miss Carrie Vincenheller, helped with the classes. McGuffey's readers and the old Blue-Back spellers were their mainstays.

On April 16, 1881, the *Echo* published Dalrymple's April report, in which those students winning honors were commended. Delia Spears and Lizzie Hourigan were awarded *distinguished,* having received the grade of 90.6; Lula Spears, Nora Spears, Howard Crawford, Etta Soule, Lucy Bennett, and Frank Conrad, Jr. *meritorious,* having grades ranging from 80 to 88.66. Dalrymple did not explain how he had arrived at these precise grades. He also gave the names of thirteen students who had attended school every day for that month.[15]

Griffin's cultural and transportation advantages, however, could not offset the boom spirit of rival towns. In February, 1881, Editor Robson, Griffin's perennial booster, accompanied H. E. Chapin on a trip through western Texas to see some of these new towns.[16] Their first stop was "Brazos City," prospective county seat of Jones County, where they found two dwellings and a "good store house," but very poor store. On the third day, they arrived at Sweetwater, "the temporary county seat of Nolan County." Here Robson interviewed a "Mr. Posey," formerly of Breckenridge, who kept "a fair stock of general merchandise." Besides this store Sweetwater had but one log house and two tents. "Five miles further on we came to Cruger and Boynton's work on the Texas and Pacific Railroad," Robson said.

Other places visited were Colorado City, Big Spring, and Abilene. Colorado City, the county seat of Mitchell County, was a better town than Sweetwater. It contained

15 "Fort Griffin as Seen through the Telescope of Memory," as cited.
16 *Fort Griffin Echo,* February 19, 1881.

two hotels and restaurants, one feed store and wagon yard, one flour and feed store, one grocery, one general merchandise, one beef market, two law offices, one doctor, five saloons, several carpenters, one printing office, "and a quantity of bummers." Although the town had a few substantial buildings, the largest being Dunn, Coleman and Company's store, most of them were of a portable kind, built in sections. Some of its citizens were, until recently, Griffinites —Judge J. F. Bozeman, proprietor of the Bozeman House; Gus Huber and John Birdwell, managers of prosperous saloons; Paul Hoefle, capitalist and speculator; and Emil Krause, a carpenter.

Hoefle accompanied Robson and Chapin on to Big Spring, in Howard County. They met here Lester E. Upham of Robson's acquaintance while in Jacksboro, who managed another of Birdwell's stores, although it was a tent store and its principal stock was "red liquor" and cigars. This was a town of only nine tents. Its principal patrons were buffalo hunters, railroad graders, and bone gatherers, with now and then a cowboy. "The place," wrote Robson, "takes its name from a beautiful spring of clear, cool water, under a huge mass of overhanging rock."

From here, he stated caustically, "we lit out for Abilene, the future great," twelve miles north of Buffalo Gap on Elm Creek, and the railroad center of Taylor County. But he had little to say about Abilene, which had become the Texas and Pacific Railroad town that Griffin had earlier aspired to be. He did state, however, that the T. & P. management there planned extensive shipping pens and intended to make Abilene the main cattle market for all the country east of the Colorado River. This town consisted of about forty houses and tents, the largest of which was occupied by Robinson Brothers, railroad supply contractors. But Robson admitted, doubtless grudgingly, that "the town bids fair to rival its Kansas namesake as a cattle mart."

Still, Abilene was not Griffin's chief rival. Griffin merchants feared Albany most. It was the county seat of Shackelford County, to which many of them moved a few years later. On February 1, 1858, Shackelford had been carved from Bosque County and was named for Dr. John Shackelford, a hero at Goliad during the Texas revolution. The county was organized on September 12, 1874, with Fort Griffin as the county seat, but in the following year the county seat was moved to the north prong of Hubbard Creek, nearer the center of the county and about fourteen miles south of Griffin.[17] The first town lots were sold on August 2, 1875, and a few months later T. E. Jackson, a Griffin businessman, built Albany's first store structure, which housed J. S. Simpson's stock of merchandise. John Jacobs erected the first residence.

Robson's visits in the new Texas and Pacific Railroad towns evidently convinced him that Griffin was hopelessly stranded as a small, inland town. He said that he had business interests elsewhere, which were more important than editing the *Echo;* therefore, his office, a quarto medium Universal press, super Royal hand press, and plenty of material were for sale. And a short time later he moved to Albany.[18]

Griffin was dealt another blow; Frank Conrad, its second most active booster, began the transfer of his business

[17] The original petition of that area's settlers to the county court of Jack County was drawn up under a fine pecan tree, about one mile from Griffin on the right bank of the Clear Fork. The petition is now in the *Albany News* office. The *Fort Griffin Echo,* March 1, 1879, reprinted it.

[18] *Fort Griffin Echo,* February 26, 1881.

to Albany, and with it the trail drivers' trade. In 1882, he closed his Griffin store, and at his new location began concentrating on supplying the trail drivers' and local ranchmen's needs. He proudly announced that he carried at Albany the largest stock of merchandise west of Fort Worth.

After 1881, Griffin dwindled rapidly. Within a few years half of the business houses became vacant. No longer did drunken Tonks stalk about the streets, for in 1884 they were moved back to Indian Territory. By the end of the century only a combination general store and post office was maintained and finally it, too, was abandoned, and the Flat faded into oblivion.

Index

Index

Conrad and Rath, frontier mercantile firm: 150, 199

Cook, John R., tells of Indian raids: 180n., 181ff.

Cowboys, of the old West: 141ff., 146–47

Crime, at Fort Griffin: 146–48

Cruger, Henry: 140

Dallas Daily Herald: 151ff.

Dalrymple, Col. W. C., at Camp Cooper: 30–31

Dalrymple, W. S., teacher: *ix*, 204–205

Davidson, Lt. Col. John B., in Indian war: 113

Davis, Gov. E. J.: complains at Indian atrocities, 77; commutes Indians' sentence, 84; deprecates Indian trials, 106

Davis, Jefferson: 4

Deno, Lottie, mysterious frontier character: 134–38

Dodge, Mr. and Mrs. Ed: *x*

Dodge, Nancy: 10

Dodge City, Kansas, terminus of cattle trail: 145

Dodge City Times, quoted: 188

Doña Ana, New Mexico, road to: 6

Drought, along the Clear Fork: 22

Earp, Wyatt, frontier peace officer: 194

Elm Creek, Young County settlement: raided by Indians, 43–44

Esa-tai, Quahada Comanche medicine man: 109

"Fandangle," of Albany, Texas: *x*

Farming, experimental: 10n.

Fort Belknap, Texas: established, 3n.; visited by Marcy, 4; subpost of Fort Griffin, 68; abandoned, 64; visited by Sherman, 80

Fort Chadbourne, Texas, subpost of Fort Griffin: 68

Fort Cobb, Indian Territory: 27

Fort Davis, stockade on the Clear Fork: *viii*, 44–50

Fort Griffin, Texas (military post): *viii, ix;* established, 65ff.; sanitation problems of, 66; building material, 66–67; officers quarters, 67; morale of troops, 67; army life at, 69; fare of officers and men, 69n., 70; entertainment at, 70, 71; beef supply, 72; headquarters for Indian campaign, 112, 115; difficulties of communication with, 114; quarters, 125–26; library, 126; hospitalizes civilians, 130; military engage in feuds, 132–33; cavalry pursues Indians, 186–87; abandoned, 197; subposts of, 68

Fort Griffin (village or "Flat"): *ix;* life at, 126–27; major trading point, 128; daily scene, 128; gambling, 128; characters, 128; Main Street, 127–28; types of business, 128–29; crime, 129; population, 132; prostitution, 134; other vice, 138–39; horse racing, 139–40; profits from cattle drives, 144–46; killings, 146–48, 150–53; outlaws, 153–56; vigilance committee, 157; night life, 158–60; decline of lawlessness, 161; hotels, 149, 162; buffalo hunters' headquarters, 175ff.; types, 194; buffalo hide business at, 195; decline, 195–97; saloons, 199; business establishments, 199–200; stagecoach service,

211

Index

Jackson, Joe, buffalo hunter: 185–86

Johnson, Britt, Negro hero: 43–44, 78

Johnson, Mode and C. J., locate near Nugent, Texas: 143

Johnston, Col. Albert S.: 20n.

Jones, Horace P., interpreter: 82–83

Kelley, Frank: *x*

Ketumse, Comanche chief: 9, 14, 19, 22

Kickapoo Indians, commit murder: 11–14

Kicking Bird, Indian chief, counsels peace: 108

King, William: 39

Kiowa Indians: raid Young County, 43; make other raids, 77; prisoners released, 96

Knox and Gardner, at Old Stone Ranch: 36

Koweaka, Wichita Indian chief, death of: 8–9

Kress, Mortimer (Wild Bill), buffalo hunter: 172

Larn, John, ranchman and peace officer: location, 128; death, 157–58

Lawton, Maj. Henry W., in charge of supplies: 89–90

Leach, June: 140

Lee, Abel John, and family: killed by Indians, 94–95, 101–102

Lee, Ernest: *xi*

Lee, Mrs. Mary Custis: 22

Lee, Capt. P. L., chases Indians, 187–88

Lee, Lt. Col. Robert E.: *viii*, 32; arrives in Texas, 21n; at Camp

Cooper, 22–24; campaigns against Indians, 24

Ledbetter, Johnny, disappears: 40–42

Ledbetter, W. H.: *ix*, 36, 128

Ledbetter Salt Works: 38

Leonard, Fred: 109

Liquor, drinking at Fort Griffin: 136ff.

Lobenstein, W. C.: buffalo hide trader: 166

Lynch, J. C.: career of, 36–38; ranch holdings, 128

McClermont, Capt. Robert: 103–104

McCombs, Jacobs, and Poe, buffalo hunters: 189–93

McElderry, Henry, assistant surgeon: 67, 125, 127

McGaughey, Mr. and Mrs. John H.: *x*

McGough, Billy, visits salt works: 39–41

McKaney and Hamberg, store: 177–78

Mackenzie, Col. Ranald S.: ordered to pursue Indians, 80–81; campaigns against Comanches, 87–92; attacks village, 95–96; in Indian campaign, 113f.; seeks out Indians, 115; routs Indians, 117–18; in campaign of 1874, 119, 120, 121

Mackenzie Trail: 114

Marcy, Capt. Randolph B.: *viii*, 3n., 12; locates Indian reservation, 5n.; holds Indian council, 15–16; inspects frontier, 79–87

Masonic Lodge, Fort Griffin: 204

Matthews, John Alexander: 142

Matthews, "Uncle Joe": establishes

Fort Griffin on the Texas Frontier

home, 42; sells beef to fort, 72;
location of home, 128
Matthews, Watt: x
Matthews family: ix
Mellen, Lieut. H. B., seeks site for
post: 64
Methodists, at Fort Griffin: 204
Miles, John D., Indian agent: 123
Miles, Col. Nelson A., in Indian
war: 3, 113, 123
Millet ranch, location: 143
Mooar, John, buffalo hunter: 167
Mooar, J. Wright, buffalo hunter:
144, 165–68, 170–71
Mooar, Miss Louise: x
Mooar brothers, operate out of Fort
Griffin: 176
Myers, A. C., in buffalo trade: 166
Myers, Charley: 109

Nail, Robert: x
Neighbors, Robert S.: viii; locates
Indian reservation, 4; conciliates
Indians, 14; reports, 18;
assassinated, 27–28; complains
to army officers, 35–36
Newcomb, George: x
Newcomb, Sam: diary, 44ff.; rides
for doctor, 57; merchant, 128
Newcomb, Susan, diary: 52ff., 81
"Nigger Horse," Comanche war-
rior: 179ff., 189
Nye, Capt. W. S.: 95

O'Keefe, Tom, frontier blacksmith: 170
Opera house, at Fort Griffin: 204
Outlaws, along the Clear Fork:
141ff.

Pah-hah-yo-ko, Comanche chief: 9
Palmer, I. N.: 32

Parker, Cynthia Ann, taken from
Indians: 29–30
Parker, Quanah, leads Comanches:
85ff., 91
Parker, W. B.: 164
Pearce, Lieut. N. B.: 4
Planters House, Fort Griffin: 195
Price, James H.: 31–32

Rath, Charley, frontier business-
man: 150, 166, 169, 172
Rath City: see Reynolds City
Rattlesnakes: 22
Reed, Charley, in shooting affair:
150–53
Reed, Jim, pioneer ranchman: 143
Reynolds, Barber Watkins: moves
to Stone Ranch, 50–51; attacked
by Indians, 54–55; builds house,
142
Reynolds, Mrs. Ethel Matthews: x
Reynolds, George: drives herd to
New Mexico, 49–50; wounded
by Indians, 55–58; home of, 142
Reynolds, Sallie Matthews, marries:
142
Reynolds, W. D., residence of: 143
"Reynolds Bend Shrine": 142
Reynolds family: ix
Richardson, R. N.: x
Rister, Mrs. Mattie May: xi
Roberts, Emmett, locates near
Nugent: 143
Robson, Editor G. W.: 140, 160,
161, 197
Ross, Capt. L. S., fights Indians:
129
Rye, Edgar: 135, 136

Salt: see Ledbetter Salt Works
Sanaco, Comanche chief: 9, 18–19

214

Index

Satanta, Kiowa chief: 82ff., 84n., 99, 108
School, Fort Griffin: 204
Sebastian, Charlie: 149
Second United States Cavalry: 20n.
Sewell, Marshall, killed by Indians: 180
Seventh United States Infantry: 3
Shackelford County: *vii*, 207
Shadler, Ike: 109–10
Sheridan, Gen. Phil, directs war on Indians: 110–11
Sherman, Gen. W. T.: reviews frontier, 79–84; comments on defense policy, 81–82
Sibley, H. H., frontier army officer: *viii*, 8–9
Simonds, Vol: 38
Sixth United States Cavalry, establishes Fort Griffin: 58
Smith, Edward P., commissioner of Indian affairs: 104
Smith, Gen. E. Kirby: 32
Smith, Elizabeth Boyle ("Aunty Hank"), pioneer: 200n., 201–202
Smith, Hans ("Uncle Hank"), pioneer resident: 200n., 201–202
Smith, Jim: 181–82
Snyder, W. H. (Pete), location of: 177
Soward, Judge John Charles: 84
Spangler, Sergeant J. W., fights Indians: 29
Spring, near Givens' ranch: 35
Stagecoach service, Fort Griffin: 203–204
Stansbury, Howard: 163n.
Stem, Jesse, Indian agent: 8; confers with Indians, 9; murdered by renegade Indians, 11ff.
Stoneman, Gen. George: 32

Stone Ranch ("Old Stone Ranch"): 34, 36, 128
Stone Ranch (on the Concho): 113
Stribling, Judge C. K.: *ix*, 128
Sturgis, Lt. Col. S. D., locates post: 63n., 64
Sun Dance, Comanche: 108–109
Sunday school, organized: 46

Tafoya, José Piedad, *Comanchero:* 115–16
Tasker, Charles: 201–202
Tatum, Lawrie, Indian agent: 82; opposes peace policy, 85; abrupt with Indians, 100
Ten Bears, Comanche chief: 99
Texas Central Railroad: 198
Texas Rangers, near Fort Griffin: 157
Thomas, Maj. George H.: *viii*, 32; visits Camp Cooper, 23; escorts Indians, 27; in campaigns against Indians, 28n.
Tonkawa Indians, in Fort Griffin country: 72, 109, 208
Tree, Lieut. A. D.: 17
Twenty-second United States Infantry: 197
Twiggs, Gen. W. A., surrenders posts: 30

Van Camp, Lieut. Cornelius, in emergency: 24–25
Van Dorn, Gen. Earl: *viii*, 32
Vigilantes, in Fort Griffin country: 141ff., 155

Walker, Francis A., commissioner of Indian affairs: 99
Warren, Henry, wagon train attacked: 80ff.
Weather, Clear Fork country:

severe, 114–15; cold, 118, 119, 120; dust storms, 127; excessive rain, 127
Webb, Mr. and Mrs. Graham: *x*
Webb, Mr. and Mrs. W. G.: *x*
West, George: 181
Western Cattle Trail: 144
White Horse, Kiowa warrior: 94f.
Wichita Indians: 8–9
Wilbarger County: *viii*

Williams, J. W.: *xi*
Williams, O. W., tells of Lottie Deno: 138
Wilson, Mrs. Mary Doak: *xi*
Wood, Lester B.: *x*
Wood, Maj. W. H.: 80; commanding post, 129
Wright, Robert M., Fort Dodge sutler: 172